The Crazy Joker's Handbook

If you want to laugh – and you want to make other people laugh too – you need THE CRAZY JOKER'S HANDBOOK, a hilarious guide to how to be funny. It's packed with hundreds of jokes, riddles, April Fools, good advice and bad shaggy dog stories, all put together by that amazing mistress of merriment, the one and only Janet Rogers.

If you want to be a crazy joker you'll have to get used to living in an upside down world where everything is back to front and as crazy as can be, and this Z to A of laughter is all you need to become the craziest joker ever.

The Crazy Joker's Handbook

Janet Rogers

Illustrated by Robert Nixon

RED FOX

THE CRAZY JOKER'S HANDBOOK
A RED FOX BOOK 978 1 849 41855 3

First published in Great Britain by Beaver Books,
an imprint of Random House Children's Publishers UK
A Random House Group Company

Beaver Books edition published 1984
Red Fox edition published 2012

1 3 5 7 9 10 8 6 4 2

The Random House Group Limited supports the Forest Stewardship Council
(FSC®), the leading international forest certification organization. Our books
carrying the FSC label are printed on FSC®-certified paper. FSC is the only
forest certification scheme endorsed by the leading environmental organiza-
tions, including Greenpeace. Our paper procurement policy can be found at
www.randomhouse.co.uk/environment.

Set in Century Schoolbook by JH Graphics Ltd, Reading, Berks

Red Fox Books are published by Random House Children's Publishers UK,
61–63 Uxbridge Road, London W5 5SA

www.randomhousechildrens..co.uk
www.randomhouse.co.uk

Addresses for companies within The Random House Group Limited can be
found at: www.randomhouse.co.uk/offices.htm

THE RANDOM HOUSE GROUP Limited Reg. No. 954009

A CIP catalogue record for this book is available from the British Library.

Printed and bound by CPI Group (UK) Ltd, Croydon, CR0 4YY

Contents

Zap! Pow!

Do you know the oldest joke in the world?
It was when Eve said to Adam: 'Do you love me?' and he replied: 'Who else?'

Since that first pair ate the first apple the world has been full of jokers. In fact anybody can be a joker once they've learnt the secret, and with this book at your fingertips you can be a joker too! Within a short space of time you can have your teachers tittering, your friends guffawing, your mother in stitches and your father in fits, children chuckling, grandparents grinning, and everyone you meet will be clutching their sides with laughter when you've mastered the art.

Before you can become a joker you must learn my Ten Golden Rules for Jokers.

Rule 1
Jokers must aim to make people cry . . . with laughter, of course! Only tell jokes that *you* think are funny. If they don't make you laugh, then they won't make other people laugh.

Rule 2
Jokers must speak clearly when telling jokes so that every word can be heard. Your funniest joke could be ruined if you spoke too fast and your audience missed what you were saying.

Rule 3

The punchline of a joke is the most important part so be sure to say it slowly, and most important of all don't start telling a joke unless you remember how it finishes!

Rule 4

A joker never tells a joke that will hurt anybody's feelings.

Rule 5

A joker never tells the same joke twice to the same person, no matter how funny the joke is or how much the person laughed at it. It will never be as funny the second time round.

Rule 6

A joker always chooses the right moment to tell a joke. If your mother has just accidentally smashed her favourite vase, however much she might need cheering up a joke about having a smashing time would not go down well. If your audience isn't in the right mood even your most hilarious jokes will not make them laugh.

Rule 7

Never play practical jokes that will cause damage, make someone angry or unhappy, frighten animals, or start World War III.

Rule 8

Whether playing practical jokes or telling funny stories, a good joker will always practise, practise and practise first to make quite certain that the outcome will be as funny as possible.

Rule 9

If your jokes involve different characters speaking, practise using funny voices and pulling crazy faces so that as you tell the joke it will become even more hilarious.

Rule 10

Always keep your own joke book – a notebook in which you can write down all the new jokes you hear. Nothing is worse than hearing a really funny joke and then forgetting it a few days later!

Stick to these ten golden rules and you will be well on the way to becoming the Crazy Joker of the Year!

Why did the comedian tell the same jokes three nights running?
He didn't dare tell them standing still!

Here's a party teaser that will catch people out every time. Take a glass and three matchsticks. Place the empty glass on the table upside down, and lay the three matchsticks beside it. Now invite one of your guests to place one match on top of the glass using the other two matchsticks. With great difficulty he or she is sure to rise to the challenge and will eventually lift a matchstick up and lay it on the glass. You then announce that they have done it wrong, for you asked for the match to be laid on the *top* of the glass and they have laid it on the *bottom*!

YOU: *I haven't slept a wink these last three days*.
VICTIM: Why's that?
YOU: *Because I sleep at night!*

There are a number of challenges with matches that you can't lose either. Place ten matches on the table and ask someone to make a monkey out of them. When they fail to do so, you take the matches and arrange them like this:

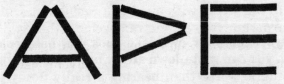

Now lay seven matches in a row on the table and challenge a friend to take away one and leave none. Can it be done? Yes, it can. Take away one match and with the six remaining matches spell the word:

NIL

Using the same seven matches, ask your friend to make a hotel with them. Obviously there aren't enough matches to spell the word hotel, but when your victim gives up you arrange them to spell the word:

INN

which is a kind of hotel. Finally, tie one matchstick on to a piece of string and announce that you will hold the string by one end and cut through it with a pair of scissors, but the matchstick will not fall to the floor. How? You tie a loop in the string and cut through that! You can't lose!

Using your piece of string, get a friend to hold an end in each hand and ask him or her to tie a knot in it, without letting go. Try as they will, they are sure to find it impossible, but you will not! Being the clever joker that you are, you simply fold your arms *then* pick up the string with an end in each hand. Unfold your arms and to everyone's amazement there will be a knot in the string and you are still holding the ends. Practise this before you challenge anyone else to do it.

Is it possible to sing under water? Yes, it is, and you can prove it too even when people say it is impossible. Simply take a glass of water and hold it above your head. Start to sing at the top of your voice and you really will be singing under water!

Ask a friend to write down the number *eleven thousand, eleven hundred and eleven* on a piece of paper. The correct answer is actually 12,111, but your victim is sure to get it wrong.

When you next have a party announce that you are a hypnotist. Ask someone to volunteer to assist you, then take a book (this one will be ideal) and say that you can place it somewhere in the room where everybody can see it *except* your assistant whom you will hypnotise. Wave your fingers in front of his or her face, and say a few magic words if you wish. Then place the book on top of your victim's head. Everybody else in the room will be able to see it, but unless your victim has eyes in the top of his head he or she will be the only one that can't.

Warning: Only perform this trick in a room without mirrors otherwise you could be made to look a fool rather than a joker, because the victim would easily be able to see the book.

You can't lose!

Fool your friends and frustrate your enemies with these tricks, bets and wheezes that you simply cannot lose!

The next time you see somebody wearing a coat, jacket or cardigan, say to them: 'I bet you can't button your coat up.'

Naturally he or she will want to prove you wrong and is certain to begin fastening the buttons. Wait until the person has finished, and then say: 'There! I knew you couldn't button your coat *up*.'

You can't lose, because everybody buttons their coat from the top *down*.

Run up to somebody at school and shout loudly:

'Hey! Your shirt tail is on fire!'

Before your victim has time to realise what is happening, you quickly pull his shirt tail out of the back of his trousers and say:

'Don't worry, it's out now!'

and then run away again . . . before he can catch you!

Take a piece of paper and challenge your friend by saying:

'I can write with my nose.'

When challenged to do so, you simply write 'with my nose' on the piece of paper!

13

YOU: *I bet I can make you say the word 'green'.*
VICTIM: I bet you can't.
YOU: *O.K., let's try. What are the colours of the Union Jack?*
VICTIM: Red, white and blue.
YOU: *There! I knew I could make you say 'green'.*
VICTIM: But I didn't say 'green'!
YOU: *You just said it!*

Here's a great game that you can play with a friend, and no matter how many times you play the game, you will never lose. Take sixteen matchsticks, cocktail sticks or pipe cleaners and lay them on the table. Your friend must then remove either one or two sticks from the table. Then it is your turn to remove either one or two sticks, and so on. The loser is the one who has to take the *last* stick from the table, but it will never be you. Your friend will always lose.

Here's how:

1 Your partner must always start first.
2 If your partner picks up one stick, you pick up *two*. If your partner takes two sticks, you take *one*.
   That way he or she will be left with the last stick every time, making you the winner.

Is it possible to show somebody something that they have *never* seen before and will *never* see again? To a crazy joker anything is possible, and this is how you do it.

You take a peanut or monkey nut, crack open the shell and swallow the nut! You have succeeded in the challenge, for nobody could ever have seen that particular nut before and it will never be seen again!

Catch someone out with this.

YOU: *What does T O spell?*

VICTIM: To.

YOU: *What does T O O spell?*

VICTIM: Too.

YOU: *And what does T W O spell?*

VICTIM: Two.

YOU: *What is the second day of the week called?*

VICTIM: Tuesday.

YOU: *Wrong! The second day of the week is Monday!*

Here's a great trick to play at a party. You need three paper cups and three sweets. Lay the sweets on the table and cover each sweet with a paper cup. Pick up the first cup and eat the sweet underneath. Then pick up the second cup and eat the sweet underneath that. Finally, pick up the third cup and eat the last sweet. Now say to a friend:

'Point to any cup and I will make sure that the three sweets are underneath it.'

Whichever cup they point to, simply balance it on your head! The three sweets are underneath it after all.

YOU: *You'd better keep your eyes open tomorrow.*

VICTIM: Why?

YOU: *Otherwise you'll bump into things!*

One of the oldest wheezes still catches people out every time. Ask the question:

'Which is correct. The yolk of an egg *is* white or the yolk of an egg *are* white?'

Your victim will probably say 'the yolk of an egg *is* white,' whereupon you will remind him that egg yolks are yellow!

Say to your friend:

'Here's a piece of paper and a pencil. I want you to write a small letter 'I' with a dot over it.'

Of course, your victim will think that is easy and is certain to write 'i' on the paper, which is wrong!

A small letter 'I' with a dot over it looks like this: i

YOU: *The Princess of Wales is going to open a new tellycost this afternoon.*
VICTIM: What's a tellycost?
YOU: *Oh, about seventy pounds.*

Xmas crackers

Christmas is a time for jokers. Last year Santa Claus went to a psychiatrist and told him that he didn't believe in himself! What I look forward to every year is pulling Christmas crackers because of the jokes inside! Here are the hundred best – or worst!

100. *Why are dentists artistic?*
    Because they're good at drawing teeth.

99. *If an egg floated down the River Thames, where would it have come from?*
    A chicken.

98. *Why did the chicken run away from home?*
    It was tired of being cooped up.

97. *What happened when the cat swallowed a penny?*
    There was some money in the kitty.

96. *Who has eight guns and terrorises the ocean?*
    Billy the Squid.

95. *Who didn't invent the aeroplane?*
    The Wrong Brothers.

94. *What would happen if pigs could fly?*
    Bacon would go up.

93. *What would you have if the cars in England were all pink?*
A pink carnation.

92. *How does a lolly get to school?*
On an icecycle.

91. *Why are brides unlucky?*
Because they never marry the best man.

90. *Why are tall people lazy?*
Because they lie longer in bed.

89. *What's chocolate on the outside, peanut on the inside, and sings hymns?*
A Sunday School Treet.

88. *What happened when the snake caught a cold?*
She adder viper nose.

87. *Why did the chicken cross the road?*
For some fowl reason.

86. *Why did the duck cross the road?*
To prove he wasn't chicken.

85. *What sort of meat do fools like?*
Chump chops.

84. *What's the difference between teachers and sweets?*
People like sweets.

83. *Why is it against the law to whisper?*
Because it isn't aloud.

82. *What gloves can be held but not worn?*
Foxgloves.

81. *Where do frogs fly flags?*
On tadpoles.

80. *When does the sea seem to be friendly?*
    When it waves.

79. *What did the policeman say to the naughty frog?*
    'Go on, hop it!'

78. *When is an envelope like a snooty person?*
    When it's stuck up.

77. *What did the bus conductor say to the one-legged man?*
    'Hop on!'

76. *What do you get if you dial: 9487320098579206441?*
    A sore finger.

75. *What happened to the kleptomaniac's daughter?*
    She took after her mother.

74. *Why do skeletons drink a lot of milk?*
    It's good for the bones.

73. *What is a forum?*
    A two-um plus two-um.

72. *What do you get if you're hit on the head with an axe?*
    A splitting headache.

71. *How do fishermen make nets?*
    They just sew a lot of holes together.

70. *If Fortune had a daughter, what would her name be?*
    Misfortune.

69. *Why is it nice being a baby?*
    It's a nappy time.

68. *Which bird is always out of breath?*
The puffin.

67. *Why did the ant elope?*
Nobody gnu.

66. *What happens if you dial 666?*
An Australian policeman arrives.

65. *When is a black dog not a black dog?*
When it's a greyhound.

64. *How was spaghetti invented?*
Somebody used his noodle.

63. *What do cats strive for?*
Purr-fection.

62. *How did the midget get into the police force?*
He lied about his age.

61. *Who tracks down lost vicars?*
The Bureau of Missing Parsons.

60. *Why did the cat join the Red Cross?*
He wanted to be a First Aid kit.

59. *What did the husband do when his wife asked
for a fur for Christmas?*
He scraped some out of the kettle.

58. *What cake is dangerous?*
Attila the Bun.

57. *What do you call pigs who live together?*
Pen friends.

56. *How do people eat cheese in Wales?*
Caerphilly.

55. *Who can shave three times a day and still have a beard?*
A barber.

54. *What did one casket say to the other casket?*
'Is that you coffin?'

53. *What did Vikings use to send secret messages?*
Norse code.

52. *What do geese watch on television?*
Duckumentaries.

51. *What fur did Adam and Eve wear?*
Bareskins.

50. *Is it bad to write on an empty stomach?*
No, but it's better to write on paper.

49. *What man claps at Christmas?*
Santapplause.

48. *If a man smashed a clock, could he be accused of killing time?*
Not if the clock struck first.

47. *What's the cheapest way to get to Australia?*
Be born there.

46. *Why couldn't the dog catch its tail?*
Because it's difficult to make ends meet these days.

45. *Why did the robber take a bath?*
So he could make a clean getaway.

44. *What happened when the lady sat on a pin?*
Nothing. It was a safety pin.

43. *What should you do if you find a gorilla sleeping in your bed?*
Sleep somewhere else.

42. *What happens if you plug your electric blanket into a toaster?*
You keep popping up all night.

41. *When is your mind like a rumpled bed.*
When it isn't made up.

40. *Why doesn't the piano work?*
Because it only knows how to play.

39. *Why couldn't anyone play cards on the ark?*
Because Noah sat on the deck.

38. *What do you do with a tree after you chop it down?*
Chop it up.

37. *Why don't scarecrows have any fun?*
Because they're stuffed shirts.

36. *Why shouldn't you tell secrets when there's a clock around?*
Because time will tell.

35. *What's the hardest thing about learning to ice skate?*
The ice.

34. *What did the bald man say when he was given a comb for Christmas?*
'I'll never part with it.'

33. *Why is mayonnaise never ready?*
Because it's always dressing.

32. *What goes 'Ho, ho, ho, plop'?*
Santa Claus laughing his head off.

31. *What form of transport gives people colds?*
A choo-choo train.

30. *What sort of children does a florist have?*
Either budding geniuses or blooming idiots.

29. *How do we know that Moses wore a wig?*
Because sometimes he was seen with Aaron and sometimes without.

28. *Why did the sheep say 'Moo'?*
She was learning a foreign language.

27. *What has four wheels and flies?*
A dust cart.

26. *What goes up in the air white, and comes down yellow and white?*
An egg.

25. *What did the tooth say to the dentist?*
'Fill 'er up!'

24. *What colour is a clear sky over Japan?*
Brew.

23. *If you don't feel well, what do you probably have?*
A pair of gloves on your hands.

22. *What has fifty legs but can't walk?*
Half a centipede.

21. *What's a bacteria?*
The rear entrance to a cafeteria.

20. *What kind of fall makes you unconscious, but doesn't hurt you?*
Falling asleep.

19. *Two men dig a hole in five days. How many days does it take them to dig half a hole?*
You can't dig half a hole!

18. *What's yellow and stupid?*
Thick custard.

17. *What's white and dashes through the desert with a bedpan?*
Florence of Arabia.

16. *Who has huge antlers and wears white gloves?*
Mickey Moose.

15. *Why should birds in a nest always agree?*
Because they might fall out.

14. *Who always succeeds?*
A toothless budgie.

13. *How do you find where a flea has bitten you?*
Start from scratch.

12. *Why did the cashier steal money from the till?*
She thought the change would do her good.

11. *What happened to the man who bought a paper shop?*
It blew away.

10. *When are eyes not eyes?*
When the wind makes them water.

9. *What did the trampoline performer say?*
'Life has its ups and downs, but I always bounce back.'

8. *How many legs does a dog have if you call its tail a leg?*
   Only four. Calling a tail a leg doesn't make it one.

7. *Why is studying mummies so interesting?*
   You get wrapped up in them.

6. *Why did the astronomer hit himself on the head in the afternoon?*
   Because he wanted to see stars during the day.

5. *Some ducks were walking down a path.*
   There was a duck in front of two ducks,
   a duck behind two ducks,
   a duck between two ducks,
   How many ducks were there altogether?
   Three ducks waddling in single file.

4. *August was the name of a puppy who was always picking on animals larger than himself. One day he got into an argument with a lion. The next days was the first of September. Why?*
Because that was the last of August.

3. *What's the craziest clock of all?*
A cuckoo clock.

2. *What has two arms, two wings, two tails, three heads, three bodies and eight legs?*
A man riding a horse and carrying a chicken.

1. *Why does Santa Claus have a garden?*
Because he likes to hoe, hoe, hoe.

Have fun at Christmas by writing your favourite jokes on pieces of paper and putting them inside your own Christmas crackers. They are much cheaper than shop-bought crackers, and can be a source of great amusement too. You can even put a potty poem inside:

On a frosty Christmas Eve
When cruising through the air,
What Santa really needs
Is thermal underwear.
But when he goes down a chimney
Towards the fire we tend
Asbestos pants for Santa
Would be better in the end!

Waiter! Waiter!

Some of the tastiest jokes on the menu are still those oldies but goodies, the 'Waiter! Waiter!' jokes. Have a feast with this selection . . . .

'Waiter, waiter, there's a button in my salad.'
'It must have fallen off while the salad was dressing.'

'Waiter, waiter, the food here is dreadful. Bring me the manager.'
'I can't, sir, he's out to lunch.'

'Waiter, waiter, what do I have to do to get a glass of water in this place?'
'Set yourself on fire, sir.'

'Waiter, waiter, this coffee's weak.'
'What do you expect me to do – give it weight training?'

'Waiter, waiter, this lobster you've brought me only has one claw.'
'It was in a fight, sir.'
'Then bring me the winner.'

'Waiter, waiter, this coffee tastes like cocoa.'
'I'm sorry, sir, I've given you tea.'

'Waiter, waiter, you've got your thumb on my steak.'
'Well, I don't want it to fall on the floor again.'

'Waiter, waiter, is this a lamb chop or a pork chop?'
'Can't you tell the difference?'
'No, I can't.'
'Then what does it matter?'

'Waiter, waiter, a cup of coffee without cream please.'
'I'm afraid we're out of cream. Would you like it without milk?'

'Waiter, waiter, I'll have a hamburger.'
'With pleasure.'
'No, with tomato sauce.'

'Waiter, waiter, how long have you worked here?'
'Only two weeks, sir. Why?'
'You can't be the one that took my order then.'

'Waiter, waiter, your tie is in my soup.'
'Don't worry, sir. It won't shrink.'

'Waiter, waiter, bring me a glass of milk and a piece of fish.'
'Fillet?'
'Yes, right to the top of the glass.'

'Waiter, waiter, there's a dead beetle in my wine.'
'Well, you did ask for something with a little body in it.'

'Waiter, waiter, there's no chicken in this chicken pie.'
'You won't find any shepherds in the shepherds pie either.'

'Waiter, waiter, do you have frog's legs?'
'No, sir. It's rheumatism makes me walk like this.'

'Waiter, waiter, I won't have any mushrooms today. I was nearly poisoned with them last week.'
'Is that so? Then I won the bet with our chef.'

'Waiter, waiter, there's a fly in my soup.'
'Don't worry – the spider on your bread roll will get it.'

'Waiter, waiter, there's a stick in my soup.'
'Yes, sir – this restaurant has branches everywhere.'
'Waiter, waiter, why does my cup of tea have a fly in it?'
'What did you expect for twenty pence – an elephant?'

'Waiter, waiter, today I'd like my soup without.'
'Without what, sir?'
'Without your thumb in it.'

'Waiter, waiter, what's the meaning of this fly in my teacup?'
'I'm a waiter, madam, not a fortune teller.'

'Waiter, waiter, you're not fit to serve a pig.'
'I'm trying my best, sir.'

'Waiter, waiter, what is this soup?'
'It's bean soup.'
'I don't care what it's been – what is it now?'

'Waiter, waiter, there's a fly in my soup.'
'Hang on a minute – I'll call the RSPCA.'

'Waiter, waiter, this soup is disgusting.'
'No, sir, it's oxtail.'

'Waiter, waiter, you've got your thumb in my soup.'
'Don't worry, sir, it's not hot.'

'Waiter, waiter, there's a fly in my butter.'
'There can't possibly be.'
'I tell you there is!'
'No there isn't – we only serve margarine.'

'Waiter, waiter, a dog just ran off with my steak!'
'Yes, it's very popular.'

'Waiter, waiter, have you smoked salmon?'
'No, but I once smoked a pipe.'

'Waiter, waiter, what do you recommend for my lunch?'
'Slimming pills by the size of your stomach.'

'Waiter, waiter, do you have pig's trotters?'
'No, it's these new shoes make me walk like this.'

'Waiter, waiter, there's a dead fly in my soup.'
'Yes, it's the heat that kills them.'

'Waiter, waiter, do you ever change the table cloths here?'
'I wouldn't know, I've only worked here a year.'

'Waiter, waiter, may I have a table for dinner?'
'Would you like it boiled or roasted, sir?'

'Waiter, waiter, this plate is damp.'
'That's the soup, sir.'

'Waiter, waiter, that crust on the steak and kidney pie was tough.'
'You've eaten the plate, sir.'

'Waiter, waiter, this egg is bad.'
'I only laid the table.'

'Waiter, waiter, I can't eat this.'
'Why not, sir?'
'You haven't given me a knife and fork.'

'Waiter, waiter, what's this in my soup?'
'I've no idea. All insects look the same to me.'

'Waiter, waiter, the butter's got sand in it!'
'That stops it slipping off the bread, sir.'

'Waiter, waiter, there's a dead fly in my soup.'
'Oh, and he was so young to die. Sob! Sob!'

'Waiter, waiter, there's a flea in my soup.'
'Shall I tell him to hop it?'

'Waiter, waiter, do the band play requests?'
'Yes, sir.'
'Well, tell them to play cards until I've finished my lunch.'

'Waiter, waiter, I think I'd like a little game today.'
'Draughts or tiddley-winks?'

'Waiter, waiter, do you call this a three-course meal?'
'That's right, sir, two chips and a pea.'

'Waiter, waiter, what's this fly doing in my soup?'
'Trying to get out, sir.'

'Waiter, waiter, can I have my bill, please.'
'How did you find your steak, sir?'
'Oh, I just moved a sprout and there it was.'

'Waiter, waiter, aren't there any menus in this place?'
'No, sir.'
'How do I know what you have?'
'Just look at the table cloth and guess.'

'Waiter, waiter, what do you call this?'
'Cottage pie, sir.'
'Well, I think I've just bitten a piece of the brickwork.'

'Waiter, waiter, there's a dead beetle in my soup.'
'Yes, sir, they're terrible swimmers.'

'Waiter, waiter, do you serve crabs?'
'We serve anybody, sir. Sit down.'

'Waiter, waiter, if this is cod, I'm an idiot!'
'You're right, sir – it is cod.'

'Waiter, waiter, there's a worm on my plate.'
'That's a sausage, sir.'

CHALLENGE!

Now that you've seen the cream of 'Waiter!' jokes, the very next time you are in a restaurant I dare you to ask the waiter a question such as, 'Do you serve crabs?' and see the result!

Video fun

'I hear you've started playing video games.'
'Yes, the doctor told me I should get some more exercise.'

In this space-age, computer-filled world in which we live, video games are all the rage, but, unless you happen to be a very rich joker, a good video game could cost you several years' pocket money, which is no joke! Never fear! With the aid of an ordinary television set, or even just a radio, you can create your own video fun.

Classroom capers

An hilarious game can be played using an ordinary radio and your own powers of story telling! Sit all the players in a circle. The first player holds the radio (preferably a small transistor that can be passed around easily) and tunes into a station which has only people talking and no music. Once the station has been found, the radio set should be turned off and the game can begin.

The player with the radio starts to tell a story about a day at school, using the names of teachers and pupils that everybody knows. When any character in the story speaks the player switches the radio on for a few seconds, and whatever the person on the radio says at that point will prove to be hilarious. For

34

example, the story might go something like this:

'It was a Monday morning, and Mr Morris, the French master, bumped into Miss Jones, the maths teacher, and said (*switch radio on*) 'There will be gales and thunderstorms in the Scilly Isles.' (*radio off*). She took off her glasses and said (*radio on*) 'The new vaccine to prevent this terrible disease should be available next year.' (*radio off*). When Mr Morris asked why she had removed her glasses, Miss Jones replied that it was because of (*radio on*) 'strong winds in the Cairngorms.' (*radio off*).'

And so the game continues. At any point the player can pass the radio on to the person next to him, who must then continue the story. The radio only needs to be switched on for a few seconds each time just so that you hear one sentence. You will soon be expert at doing this, and the results can be very funny indeed.

Mime time

The above game can, of course, be played using a television set (but do get permission from an adult before you touch the television). There are other games that you can play with a television set too. The first is for the players to sit around the set with the volume turned down, and each player can choose to be a character that is appearing in the programme. Each time your character appears on the screen and opens his or her mouth you must speak at the same time with what you think that person might be saying. The art of the game is to speak at exactly the same time as the character moves his lips, and to stop when he or she stops. If you end your sentence at exactly the point when the character stops speaking, give yourself five points. The player with the most points at the end of the programme is the winner.

Another good game to play is that of lip-reading. The players must sit around the set with the volume turned down and take it in turns to play. To play the game you must watch the person speaking on television very closely , look at their lips and try to work out what you think they are talking about. After one minute turn the volume up and see if you are right. You might, for example, think that you see the speaker say the word 'ship-building' several times, and if when the volume is turned up ship-building is the topic of conversation then you will score a point. If, however, the person is talking about 'cream cakes' and is unlikely to have ever mentioned ship-building then you score nothing. Players must not cheat by looking in the *Radio Times* to see what programmes are about beforehand though!

A final television game can be played while you watch a film or play on the screen. After fifteen or twenty minutes (depending upon how long the programme is) the players should be given a piece of paper and write down how they think the story will end. The one who guesses correctly is the winner!

Ugh!

If you happen to be squeamish, afraid of ghosts and frightened by monster movies, you are of a nervous disposition and these jokes are not for you! But if you don't faint at the sight of blood, wouldn't bat an eyelid if a ghost walked through your wall and long to be a member of the Dracula Fang Club (just send your name, address and blood sample to Transylvania), then be prepared to groan and wail at these ghoulish giggles and horrible howlers!

What happens when monsters hold a beauty contest?
Nobody wins.

What kind of ship did Dracula captain?
A blood vessel.

What is ten metres long, ugly and croons 'Scotland the Brave'?
The Loch Ness Songster.

What is big and green and sits around in a corner all day?
The Incredible Sulk.

CANNIBAL WIFE: *I don't know what to make of my husband.*
FRIEND: How about a hotpot?

Why do witches ride on broomsticks?
Because vacuum cleaners are too heavy.

MAC THE MONSTER: *Hurry up with my supper!*
MRS MONSTER: Oh, be quiet! I've only got three pairs of hands.

What do you call a ghost doctor?
A surgical spirit.

Where do ghouls stay when they go on holiday?
At a ghost-house.

DRACULA'S WIFE: As we're going on holiday tomorrow, remind me to cancel our daily pint of blood.

Did you hear about the two blood cells?
They loved in vein.

FIRST GHOST: *I find haunting castles a bore these days.*
SECOND GHOST: Me too. I don't seem to be able to put any life into it.

'*Mummy, why can't we get a waste disposal unit?*'
'Shut up, and keep chewing.'

What did the vampire say after a visit to the dentist?
'Fangs very much.'

What did the monster do after the dentist pulled out a tooth?
He ate the dentist.

How do ghosts lie perfectly flat when they sleep?
They use a spirit level.

What should you do if you meet Dracula, Franken-stein's monster, four werewolfs, two vampires, and the Incredible Hulk all in one room?
Keep your fingers crossed that it's a fancy dress party.

What is a monster's favourite soup?
Scream of tomato.

A ghoul stood on a bridge one night.
Its lips were all a-quiver.
It gave a cough,
Its leg fell off
And floated down the river.

'Excuse me, your wife just fell in that well.'
'That's okay, nobody drinks water from there any more.'

How did the dentist become a brain surgeon?
His drill slipped.

FIRST GHOST: *I don't seem to frighten people any more.*
SECOND GHOST: I know. We might as well be dead for all they care.

What entertainment do ghosts enjoy at Christmas?
A trip to the phantomime.

Why couldn't the skeletons go to the ball?
They had no body to dance with.

What is a sick joke?
Something you mustn't bring up in polite conversation.

Why do demons and ghouls get on so well?
Because demons are a ghoul's best friend.

'Mummy, mummy, what's for dinner?'
'Shut up and get back in the oven.'

'I used to be a werewolf, but I'm all right nowooooooooooooooh!

Who is Tibetan, hairy and courageous?
Yak the Giant Killer.

Who is German, dangerous and a terrible actor?
Attila the ham.

What kind of music do witches play on the piano?
Hag-time.

What is creepy and plays the Top Twenty?
Tranny by Gaslight.

What is bright red and dumb?
A blood clot.

Who is short, afraid of wolves and uses bad language?
Little Rude Riding Hood.

What do ghosts eat for breakfast?
Dreaded wheat.

What did the monster say when he saw Santa Claus?
Yum, yum!

How did Frankenstien's monster eat his dinner?
He bolted it down.

Who has feathers and fangs and goes 'quack'?
Count Duckula.

'Why don't you go out and play football with your brother?'
'I'm tired of kicking him around.'

What jewels do monsters wear?
Tomb stones.

Did you hear about the girl monster who wasn't pretty and wasn't ugly?
She was pretty ugly.

What do you call a twenty-tonne monster with three heads?
Sir.

Count Dracula has denied that he is to marry Viscountess Vampire.
They are to remain just good fiends.

What do monsters do every night at 11 o'clock?
Take a coffin break.

There was an old man...

There was an old man of Nantucket
Who kept all his cash in a bucket.
    But his daughter, named Nan,
    Ran away with a man,
And as for the bucket – Nantucket!

That five-line poem is called a limerick, and people
have been writing them for hundreds of years.
Nobody really knows why they are called limericks,
but it may have some connection with Limerick in
Ireland.

Although we do not know who wrote the first
limerick, the first person to make limericks popular
was a Victorian writer called Edward Lear:

Although at the limericks of Lear
We may be tempted to sneer,
    We should never forget
    That we owe him a debt
For his work as the first pioneer.

Lear's limericks are as popular today as when he first
wrote them a hundred years ago. Here's a sample:

There was an old man from Peru
Who dreamt he was eating his shoe.
    He awoke in the night
    In a terrible fright
And found it was perfectly true.

43

You can write limericks too. The secret of writing them is that the first, second and fifth lines must rhyme together, and the third and fourth lines should end with words that rhyme too. To practise, here are a couple of limericks for you to complete . . .

> There once was a boy from Rumania
> Who . . .
>
> There was a young lady from Hull
> Who . . .
>
> A man with a very large nose
> Said . . .
>
> There was an old man with a beard
> Who said . . .

Now here are some of my favourite limericks –

> There was a young lady named Rose
> Who had a big wart on her nose.
> When she had it removed
> Her appearance improved
> But her glasses slipped down to her toes.
>
> There once was a fat boy called Kidd
> Who ate twenty cream cakes for a quid.
> When asked: 'Are you faint?'
> He replied: 'No, I ain't,
> But I don't feel as well as I did.'
>
> There was a young lady of Lynn
> Who was so uncommonly thin
> That when she essayed
> To drink lemonade,
> She slipped through the straw and fell in.

There was an old man known as Keith
Who sat on his set of false teeth.
    Said he with a start,
    'Oh dear, bless my heart!
I have bitten myself underneath!'

A professor named Aubrey Brett
Said 'Three things I always forget,
    There's all my friend's names,
    And the times of the trains,
And the third one I can't recall yet!'

There was a young man from Bengal
Who went to a fancy-dress ball.
    He said he would risk it
    And went as a biscuit,
But a dog ate him up in the hall.

Sweet little Emily Rose
Was tired and sought some repose,
   But her sister named Clare
   Put a pin on her chair,
And sweet little Emily Rose!

There was a young lady named Perkins
Who was so very fond of gherkins.
   One day at tea
   She ate fifty three
And pickled her internal workings.

I sat next to the duchess at tea
And it was just as I feared it would be.
   Her rumblings abdominal
   Were simply phenomenal,
And everyone thought it was me!

There once was a gnu in a zoo
Who tired of the same daily view.
   To seek a new sight
   He stole out one night
And where he went gnobody gnu.

Sing something silly

Do you ever sing silly songs at school? You know, the kind where you take a well-known song or nursery rhyme and put your own words to it. I bet at some time or another you've sung:

> 'Happy birthday to you,
> Squashed tomatoes and stew ...'

haven't you? I know that when I was at school, every Christmas we used to sing:

> 'While Shepherds washed their socks by night
> All seated round the tub,
> The Angel of the Lord came down
> And gave them all a scrub.'

Here are some more popular versions, but I'm sure you can invent lots of your own!

> Little Jack Horner
> Sat in a corner
> Eating his Christmas pie;
> He put in his thumb
> But instead of a plum,
> He squirted fruit juice in his eye!

> Little Miss Muffet
> Sat on her tuffet,
> But nobody said 'Hello'.
> Then down came a spider
> Who sat down beside her,
> And told Miss Muffet about her B.O.

Roses are red,
Violets are blue.
Sugar is sweet
And expensive too.

Jack and Jill went up the hill
To fetch a pail of water.
Jack fell down and broke his crown,
And sued the farmer and his daughter.

Mary had a little lamb,
A lobster and some prunes,
A glass of wine, a piece of tart,
And a plate of macaroons;
She also had two large cream cakes,
A portion of cod's roe;
And when they carried Mary out
Her face was white as snow.

Ding dong bell.
Pussy's in the well.
But we've put some disinfectant down,
And don't care about the smell.

Here's the joker's Top Ten in the Hit Parade!

1. 'I TALK TO THE TREES' Which interests my psychiatrist.
2. 'I CAN'T GIVE YOU ANYTHING BUT LOVE' The Scotsman's pop song.
3. 'ARE YOU LONESOME TONIGHT?' Try using a deodorant.
4. 'IF YOU WERE THE ONLY GIRL IN THE WORLD' You'd still be lonely.
5. 'I GET A KICK OUT OF YOU' Please sell that donkey of yours.

6. 'HAPPY DAYS ARE HERE AGAIN' It must be the school holidays.
7. 'IF I HAD A TALKING PICTURE OF YOU' I'd put a piece of sticking plaster over its mouth.
8. 'I'VE GOT YOU UNDER MY SKIN' I thought it was crowded in here.
9. 'WHEN THE MIDNIGHT CHOO-CHOO LEAVES FOR ALABAM' It will be three hours late.
10. 'CAN THIS BE LOVE?' No, it's indigestion.

> Mary had a little lamb
> As dirty as a hog.
> They asked her how it got that way,
> She simply answered: 'Smog.'

Daisy, Daisy,
Where is the Irish Stew?
You're so lazy,
What are we going to do?
We'll go hungry, I've a hunch,
'Cos we can't afford the lunch,
So we'll have to cheat
And suck on a sweet,
And pretend that we've eaten stew!

Humpty Dumpty sat on a wall.
Humpty Dumpty had a great fall.
All the King's horses
And all the King's men
Had scrambled eggs for breakfast again.

Little Bo Peep has lost her sheep
And looks for them sedately.
I hope that she will find them soon;
We've had no lamb chops lately.

Read all about it!

Jokers must communicate with each other to pass on new jokes, and what better form of communication is there than a newspaper? Why not start your own newspaper? It can be a weekly edition put together with your friends and fellow jokers. As it's your very own newspaper you can put in it exactly what you like – drawings, cartoons, humorous horoscopes, nutty news, crazy quizzes and crosswords, and lots and lots of jokes! First choose a title for your paper. How about:

'THE DAILY JOKER'
'JOKER'S WORLD'
'THE JOKER'S BUGLE'?

Then you are ready to begin!

Headlines

All newspapers have headlines and here are some of the craziest that have appeared in *real* newspapers!

AUTHOR BLAMES PRINTER FOR BAD
SPEELING

MAN FOUND DEAD IN GRAVEYARD

FALSE CHARGE OF THEFT OF HENS – POLICE
ON A WILD GOOSE CHASE

DEFECTIVE SERGEANT LEAVES THE FORCE

HOTEL BURNS DOWN: 200 HALF GLAD GUESTS ESCAPE

MOTORIST HEAVILY PENALISED – SUSPENDED FROM WHEEL FOR A YEAR

MAN RECOVERING AFTER FATAL ACCIDENT

UNDERTAKER'S FAILURE – LET DOWN BY CUSTOMERS

PASSENGERS HIT BY CANCELLED TRAINS

GASMEN GRILLED BY VILLAGERS

TWENTY-YEAR FRIENDSHIP ENDS AT THE ALTAR

POLICE WITH TRACKER DOGS HAVE SO FAR FAILED TO FIND A LEAD

GIRL HAD A DETECTIVE IN HER BOOT

PRISONERS ESCAPE AFTER EXECUTION

UNLESS THE TEACHERS RECEIVE A HIGHER SALARY THEY MAY DECIDE TO LEAVE THEIR PESTS

HECKLER TRIED TO RUIN PLAY BUT ACTORS SUCCEEDED

MEMBERS OF PARLIAMENT ACT TO KEEP THEATRES OPEN

Here is the news

Newspapers must, of course, reveal what is happening in this crazy world . . .

'A lorry load of hair restorer has been spilt on the M4. Police are combing the area.'

'We are sorry to announce that Mr Albert Perkins has been quite unwell, owing to his recent death, and is taking a short holiday to recover.'

'Eleven tents were pitched and nearly twenty youngsters converged on the camping site. Wood was chopped and a general purpose fire under Mr Tom Watkins, and the drizzly atmosphere was soon flavoured with the scent of wholesome sizzling.'

'Princess Alexandra today pressed a button and unveiled a plague to mark the opening of the new reservoir.'

'Six beds have been stolen from a warehouse. Police say they will spring into action.'

'Last night somebody drilled a hole in the fence surrounding a nudist camp. Police are looking into it.'

'Mr & Mrs Hector Draycott wish to announce that the baptism of their daughter Henry William will take place on Saturday 14th May at St Mary's Church.'

'The secretary agreed that as normal a Christmas Eve ball would be held. It was decided to hold the ball on 24th December.'

'The Misses Vivian, Lily May and Dorothy Smith are spending some time at the home of their mother, Mrs Agnes Smith. This is the first time the village has had the pleasure of seeing the girls in the altogether for more than ten years.'

'A villain escaped from prison by helicopter yesterday. Police have set up road blocks, but have so far failed to find him.'

'A lorry carrying treacle has overturned on the A35. Police have asked motorists to stick to their own lanes.'

'British Rail are looking into the idea of improving the train service between London and Luton by making more trains stop at Luton.'

'Undertakers will stage an annual exhibition at Wembley. It will take place in the week following the Hearse of the Year Show.'

It pays to advertise

In your newspaper you must include some small ads. Here are some genuine announcements and advertisements, just to give you an idea!

FOR SALE Six kittens -- fond of mousework!

PRIZE COW Come and see Mrs Dobson for fresh milk.

YOUNG LADY wants washing and cleaning three times a week.

DECORATOR specialises in inferior work.

INFLATABLE RUBBER DINGHY FOR SALE Good as new. £5. Slight puncture.

WANTED experienced carpenter to help make antiques.
CORK NOTICEBOARDS FOR SALE You can't pin anything on our goods.
WIDOWS MADE TO ORDER Send us your measurements.

SAW MILL manager requires extra hands.

HELP WANTED Man to handle dynamite. Must be prepared to travel unexpectedly.

An unexpected vacancy has occurred for a knife-thrower's assistant. Rehearsals start immediately in preparation for Milton Keynes City Show.

Alligator for sale. Would exchange for wooden leg.

DRIVING SCHOOL Crash courses given.

WANTED reliable young woman to cook, wash, iron and milk two cows.

Quick fire

A good joker will not only tell jokes to be funny, but will punctuate everyday conversation with quick quips and witty remarks. Amaze your family, flaw your friends, and amuse everybody with these quick-fire jokes. Every morning when you get up, learn one or two of these quips and soon you'll be able to sprinkle your conversation with laughter-making lines, like these:

I can't understand why it's still raining. The holidays are over.

It's time to get your shoes re-soled if, when you step on a coin, you can tell whether it's heads or tails.

I love sunshine. I could sit in the sun day and night.

Watch out when ordering in a fancy restaurant. If you can't pronounce it, you can't afford it.

You think you have troubles? My sundial is slow!

Everyone should have at least two friends. One to talk to and one to talk about.

I'm glad I wasn't born in France. I can't speak a word of French.

I'm so clumsy that if I fell down, I'd probably miss the floor.

Today I wrote three letters. A, B and C.

I don't think I'm wanted. I asked my parents for something to play with in the bath and they bought me a piranha fish!

Our family is so ugly, we keep the negatives in the photograph album.

I live in a rough area. At Christmas I hung my stocking up and Santa Claus stole it.

If you have a headache, thrust your head through a window and the pane will disappear.

It was so hot, the chickens were laying hardboiled eggs.

He died a natural death – he was hit by a car.

I asked my girlfriend if I could see her home, so she got out a photograph.

I was going to give my mother a box of chocolates for her birthday, but I'm on a diet.

I can only boil eggs for five seconds. If I hold my hand in boiling water any longer it hurts.

If evolution really worked, we'd have more than one pair of hands.

I'm thinking of becoming a doctor. I've got the handwriting for it.

You can see in the paper that everybody dies in alphabetical order.

My dog is so lazy. He waits for another dog to bark, then opens his mouth.

Never give a person a book as a present. They may already have one.

Perfume sellers push their business up other people's noses.

If you want to look beautiful, stand with a crowd of ugly people.

I was a war baby. My parents took one look at me and started fighting.

Get back at the postman for slow service. Post him his Christmas present.

I'd hate to sleep in a water bed. I can't swim.

I feel as happy as a hungry flea on a fat dog.

Never walk away from a fight. Run away from it.

Prevent a head cold from going to your chest. Tie a knot in your neck.

I gave her a going-away present, but she never did.

I'm sure we've met before. I don't remember your name, but I never forget a dress.

Rabbits' feet are lucky for everybody – except rabbits.

I sing a lot for charity. I have to. Nobody will pay me.

I know someone who's taken so many iron pills, he's starting to go rusty.

Never put off until tomorrow what you can put off for good.

The best way to cure insomnia is to get lots of sleep.

Let's wash the windows, Mother. The neighbours are straining their eyes.

She has a soft heart and a head to match.

I come home from school and smell a delicious meal cooking in the kitchen. I know one thing immediately – I'm in the wrong house.

The best way to get ahead is to have one.

As the strong man said on his way to the beach: 'I'm mussel-bound!'

A pen can be driven but a pencil is better when it's lead.

Our kitchen is so small we can only use condensed milk.

Did you hear about the man who worked in a loony bin? The people he met were just crazy about him.

My Dad is so old, when he was at school history was called current events.

I call my dog Camera because he's always snapping.

An apple a day keeps the doctor away, but an onion a day keeps everybody away.

Why does Christmas always come when the shops are so crowded?

My sister can't afford make-up. Instead of eye-shadow she sticks her head up the chimney and blinks.

We're having something different for lunch today – food.

It's so foggy I can't see what the weather's like.

Have you been to the zoo? I mean as a visitor.

Don't shout at me. I'm not your mother.

I have hundreds of books, but no bookcase. Nobody seems to want to lend bookcases.

I've found a cure for seasickness. A very tight collar.

Excuse me, but are you reading that newspaper you're sitting on?

I've discovered how to hammer in nails without hitting my thumb. I get somebody else to hold the nail.

He's such an idiot he put a bucket under a gas leak.

What I want to know is, if matches are made in Heaven, why do they cost 3p a box?

I'm such a loser. Even my artificial flower died.

I speak eight languages. Unfortunately all at the same time.

I'm not afraid of the dark, as long as the light's left on.

I taught my dog to beg. Today he came back with 50p.

Going to the comedians' school was easy. All the lessons were a joke!

Old football players never die. They just kick off.

How do people get well in hospital when everybody you meet there is sick?

Big noses usually run in families.

Memory is the thing we forget with.

Be kind to your friends. If it wasn't for them you'd be a complete stranger.

Puntime

A-pun my word! It's puntime!

What is a pun? Well, a pun is when you play around with words that sound the same. Many jokes are based on puns, especially knock-knock jokes:

Knock, knock.
Who's there?
Jester.
Jester who?
Jester minute and I'll find out!

Knock, knock.
Who's there?
Dishwasher.
Dishwasher who?
Dishwasher way I spoke before I had false teeth!

Here the words 'jester' and 'dishwasher' are used as puns.
Here are some more words that can be *pun*ished!

ABSINTHE Absinthe makes the heart grow fonder.
ATCHOO Sneezing is much atchoo about nothing.
AUTHOR Author any more at home like you?
BENIGN What you can't wait to be after you are eight.
BIT Horses often feel a bit down in the mouth.
CANTICLE Jokes canticle your fancy.
CARROT This carrot to be filled up with petrol.

CATGUT Our catgut stuck in a tree.

DEBATE With which you catch defish.

DEPEND At the swimming baths don't jump in at the depend.

EARN You live and earn.

EARRING Grandma's got a new earring aid.

EDITH Edith me on the lips.

FALSIFY I balance a book on my head, but it falsify move.

FOLDER Children should always show respect folder people.

GHOUL There's no ghoul like an old ghoul.

GRAB A shoplifter has the gift of the grab.

GRUESOME Grandfather gruesome whiskers.

HARP Harp the Herald Angels sing.

HAIR Hair today and gone tomorrow.

HOLLOW He was so rude he didn't even say hollow.

ICING Icing my favourite songs.

INFLUENZA I opened the window and influenza.

JAB Jab a good fight?

JUDICIOUS Hands that judicious can be soft as your face.

JUICY Juicy what I just saw?

KAYAK You can't have your kayak and eat it.

KINDRED Fear of relatives.

LATIN It's your fault for Latin them in in the first place.

LETTUCE Lettuce have salad for tea.

LION He's lion about his age again.

METAPHOR I metaphor the first time yesterday.

MIAOW I'm learning to steal. A cat burglar is teaching miaow.

MONKEY A fool and his monkey are soon parted.

NASAL Nelson was a nasal hero.

NINNY Someone who looks after children.

OAF Half an oaf is better than none.

OPAL Opal get a bike for Christmas.

PASTA I walked pasta without realising it was her.

PICKET It will never heal if you picket.

QUILL Where there's a quill there's a way.

REBATE Put the worm back on the hook.

REDDISH I like to have a reddish in my salad.

RUTH Ruth is stranger than fiction.

SHACK It came as quite a shack to me when I
inherited that tumbledown house.

SKID Sign on a tyre shop: We Skid You Not.

SPY Can't take my spies off of you.

TANK Tank you very much.

TAUT Walking a tightrope must be taught.

TURNIP Let's plant it and see what will turnip.

UNCTION Unctions speak louder than words.

URCHIN It dribbled down urchin.

VENICE Question in Italy: 'Venice the next gondola
due?'

VERSE These may be bad puns, but they could be
verse.

WATER Water we going to do? We're flooded.

WICK Candlemakers want longer wick ends.

X If you don't know how to vote, just X someone.

Y It's important to vote, even if you don't know Y.

ZEND Zend me a letter to tell me zoo won the game.

You get the idea! Puns are not meant to be read, but
are meant to be *said*! Once you've mastered the art of
punning, you can begin to invent your own jokes.

'Help me! I'm a pauper.'
'Congratulations! Is it a boy or a girl?'

Why was the weathercock conceited?
Because he was a vane (vain) creature.

65

What is the proverb about catching a cold?
'Win a flu, lose a flu (few).'

'How can I make antifreeze?'
'Hide her woollen pyjamas.'

How do monkeys keep rumours circulating?
On the apevine.

'Do you hunt bear?'
'Never in cold weather.'

JUDGE: *Tell me, why did you steal that purse?*
PRISONER: I wasn't feeling well, Your Honour, and I
thought the change would do me good.

It isn't the cough
That carries you off.
It's the coffin
They carry you off in.

When do telephone operators like to celebrate?
Hello-een.

How do fleas travel?
By itch-hiking.

Why did Dracula keep his coffin in a vault?
He liked to have vaulty winks.

What do Chinese cannibals eat with?
Chap-sticks.

What is an icon?
Something that grows on oak trees!

TEACHER: *Can you tell me the nationality of Napoleon?*
WILLIAM: Course I can.
TEACHER: *That's correct.*

What is a crick?
The noise a Japanese camera makes.

What did the rabbit want to do when it grew up?
Join the Hare force.

Why did the cannibal decide to become a missionary?
'If you can't eat 'em, join 'em!'

'Do you sing Faust?
'Yes, and I can also sing slow.'

'Did I ever tell you about my forebears?'
'No, but you once told me about the three bears.'

Where did King Arthur go for entertainment?
To a knight club.

On what day of the year did soldiers start wars in history?
March forth.

Do zombies like being dead?
Of corpse!

When do ghosts have to stop scaring people?
When they lose their haunting (hunting) licences.

Why is a shoemaker like a clergyman?
Both try to save soles (souls).

Where is the headquarters of the Umpires' Association?
The Umpire State Building.

'Why were you hanging around after that steamroller accident?'
'I was just scraping up an acquaintance.'

Odes and ends

Here are some potted poems and terse verse to recite
aloud . . .

I shot a sneeze into the air.
It fell to earth. I know not where.
But some time later, so I'm told,
Twenty others caught my cold.

Mary had a little lamb,
You've heard this tale before.
But did you know
She passed her plate
And had a little more?

Old Tom is gone (too soon alas!)
He tried to trace escaping gas.
With lighted match he braved the fates
Which blew him to the Pearly Gates.

It doesn't breathe; it doesn't smell;
It doesn't feel so very well.
I am disgusted with my nose.
The only thing it does is blows.

My Bonnie leaned into the gas tank,
But nothing could she see;
She lighted a match to assist her –
Oh, bring back my Bonnie to me.

Down the street his funeral goes
As sobs and wails diminish.
He died from drinking varnish,
But he had a lovely finish.

'Your teeth are like the stars,' he said,
And pressed her hand so white.
He spoke the truth, for like the stars,
Her teeth came out at night.

Newton heard a sort of plonk.
An apple fell upon his conk.
Discovering gravitation's law
Shook old Isaac to the core.

'Twas in a restaurant they met,
Romeo and Juliet.
He had no cash to pay the debt
So Romeo'd while Juliet.

A painter who lived in West Ditting
Interrupted two girls with their knitting.
He said with a sigh,
'That park bench – well, I
Just painted it, right where you're sitting!'

I shot an arrow in the air.
It fell to earth, I know not where.
I lose all my arrows that way.

One fine day in the middle of the night
Two dead men got up to fight.
Back to back they faced each other,
Drew their swords and shot each other.
A frozen donkey, passing by,
Kicked a blind man in the eye,
Knocked him through a six inch wall
Into a ditch and drowned them all.

Here I sit in the moonlight,
Abandoned by women and men,
Muttering over and over,
I'll never eat garlic again.

The squirrel has a bushy tail;
The possum's tail is bare;
The rabbit has no tail at all,
Just a little tuft of hair.

There was once a fellow named Anthony Gray,
Who ate apples all night
And ate apples all day.
He's in hospital now,
That's what they say,
And a doctor a day keeps the apple away.

When I die, bury me deep.
Bury my history book at my feet.
Tell the teacher I've gone to rest
And won't be back for the history test.

The baker's wife, Alberta Smythe,
Had loads and loads of fun,
For every time she did her hair
She put it in a bun.

I had written to Aunt Maud,
Who was on a trip abroad,
When I heard she'd died of cramp –
Just too late to save the stamp.

I've travelled on the ocean,
I've wandered over the plain,
But I've never seen a window cry
Because it had a pane.

72

The bottle of perfume that Willie sent
Was highly displeasing to Millicent.
Her thanks were so cold
They quarrelled, I'm told,
Through that silly scent Willie sent Millicent.

History's a dreadful subject,
Dead as it can be.
Once it killed the Romans
And now it's killing me.

I love you, I love you,
Please be my Valentine.
And give me your bubble gum,
'Cos you're sitting on mine!

Doctor Bell fell down the well
And broke his collarbone.
Doctors should attend the sick
And leave well alone.

No nonsense

There's more to being a joker than simply telling jokes and making people laugh. Once you've gathered together a collection of jokes, why not put on your very own comedy show just like a real comedian?

If you are going to do a complete show – perhaps lasting half an hour – why not get some friends to help you as well? To make your show as much fun and as exciting as possible, each person in the show should choose to be a certain character such as a clown, a cowboy, a doctor, a teacher, a nurse, a mad professor or a zany magician.

Once you have decided on a character, you can then collect together jokes that would suit that character. A doctor character could tell jokes concerned with the medical profession and build up an act using those jokes. For example:

'I was in my surgery today and a woman came in to see me. She was in a terrible panic, and said that I must see her husband. She was worried about him because he seemed to think he was a lorry. I said:

"Send him in to see me straight away."

"I can't," she replied. "He's gone to Newcastle to deliver some ten-tonne steel girders."

'Another man came to see me because his eyesight was failing. I told him that carrots are good for the eyes, but he said he nearly went blind everytime he stuck them in.'

Simply string all your jokes together in this way to form a short act. You could dress as a waiter or waitress carrying a tray and tell all those funny restaurant jokes, or dress in an outrageous costume and recite some potty poems. If each person taking part in your comedy show takes on the role of a different character and tells a particular kind of joke, you can soon put together a hilarious show with which to entertain your family and friends.

Two people together can form a double act and tell quick-fire gags and ridiculous riddles, one asking the question:

'What did one tap say to the other?'

and the partner giving the answer:

'You're a big drip!'

Or you can vary it, like this:

'I say, I say, I say. What did the Eskimo's wife sing when her husband asked her what she was cooking for supper?'

'I don't know, what did the Eskimo wife sing when her husband asked her what she was cooking for supper?'

'Whale meat again . . .' (*sing*)

Once you have decided which jokes to tell, learn them off by heart and practise them over and over again until you are word perfect. Practise your funny voices and silly walks too – anything that will help to make your comedy show really hilarious.

Next, gather together your costume. A baggy suit, a silly hat and a red nose will do for a clown, a white

75

jacket splattered with red paint (to look like blood) for a doctor, and so on.

Finally, you need to decide on a time and place for your comedy show. Perhaps if you have a large lounge at home you could perform your show there. Put all the chairs down one end for your audience to sit, and the performers could stand at the other and do their act, like a mini theatre. Make sure the door is at the 'stage' end of the room so that the comedians can come in and out in turn. Send out invitations to all your family and friends (who are not performing), letting them know the time and place of your show. The larger your audience, the more fun you will have.

To make your show really professional, use a tape recorder to play some music before the show, and perhaps a quick burst between each act, such as a fanfare or drum roll. If you have one person who can take charge of this, then so much the better.

On the night of your show, get all your performers together early and dressed in their costumes well before the show and keep them out of the way of the audience until the show begins. You can all practise your acts while you wait.

Once the show begins, keep it moving fast so that while one act is on the next person is standing by ready to come on and then the pace of the show will be smart, crisp and professional. To make the show a big success, remember these rules:

- Speak loudly and clearly so that your audience can hear every single word.

- If you forget a joke, don't panic, just go straight on to the next one.

- Always say the punchline of your joke slightly slower than the rest of the joke so that the audience get the full impact, and pause afterwards for a few seconds, because if your jokes are really funny the audience will want to laugh or clap.

- However well your show goes, and however much the audience laugh, don't be tempted to go on and on. It's much better to have a half-hour show that is enjoyed by all than a two-hour show that is endured.

Remember, practice makes perfect. Don't perform a show unless you feel happy about telling the jokes, and most important of all – enjoy yourself! After a few shows for your family, you might then be able to move on to telling jokes in school concerts or at your local youth club, and soon you'll be the joker everybody wants to hear!

Multi-storey stories

Here are ten of the tallest tales I've ever heard!

A rabbit was walking down the road when he suddenly felt very hungry. Just over the road was a public bar, so the rabbit walked in and asked the barman if they served food.

'Yes, we do,' replied the barman. 'Today we are serving toasties. There are cheese toasties, tomato toasties, ham toasties, pickle toasties . . .'

'That sounds great,' said the rabbit. 'I'll have a pint of shandy and a ham toastie.'

The rabbit took his drink and this toastie and went and sat in the corner. He finished his toastie but still felt hungry, so he went back to the bar and ordered another drink and a tomato toastie. He took these back to the table and devoured them hungrily. Still feeling hungry, he went back to the bar and ordered yet another drink and a cheese toastie and returned to his seat.

By now the drink had gone to his head and the rabbit appeared to be very drunk. The barman didn't like this and so decided that he must throw the rabbit out. He walked up to the rabbit and told him to stand up, but as the rabbit did so he fell down dead on the floor. The barman was very embarrassed and not wanting the other customers to see, he quickly took the rabbit outside and buried him.

The barman forgot all about the rabbit, but that evening he was serving in the bar again when suddenly the ghost of the rabbit walked through the wall causing everybody to scream with horror. The barman was stuck behind the bar and could not escape, so nervously he asked:

'Was there anything wrong with your drink?'

'No,' replied the rabbit.

'What caused you to die then?'

'Mixin' matoasties,' replied the rabbit.

A boy had been climbing a tree in the garden when he tore his trousers. His mother said, 'Now, Harold, I want you to go upstairs, take off your trousers so that I can mend them, and stay in your bedroom until dinner time.'

Fifteen minutes later, Harold's mother heard a noise coming from the cellar. She thought that Harold had disobeyed her, had come down from his room and was now playing in the cellar. She shouted,

'You are a naughty boy! Are you running around down there without any trousers on?'

A man's deep voice came from the cellar,

'No, madam, I just came to read the electricity metre.'

Two men were riding in a train for the very first time in their lives, and to sustain them on their journey they had brought along a bunch of bananas. After a while they began to feel hungry and decided that it was time to have a banana each. Just as they began to peel their bananas, the train entered a long dark tunnel.

'Have you eaten your banana yet?' cried the first man.

'No,' replied his friend.

'Well, don't touch it!' warned the first man. 'I took one bite and went blind.'

There was once a boy who found a magic lamp, and when he rubbed it, out popped a genie.

'I grant you three wishes,' said the genie.

'My first wish,' said the boy, 'is for a magic bottle of lemonade. When you pour it out the bottle fills up again.'

'Your wish has been granted,' said the genie, and the boy received a bottle of lemonade and an empty glass. He poured himself a glass and the bottle automatically filled itself again. He poured another glass, and the same thing happened.

'It works!' cried the delighted boy. 'I'll have another two bottles!'

One day a zoo-keeper had to go to the airport to collect a crate of penguins which had just arrived. The zoo-keeper had a van, so he collected the penguins and put them in the back of his van and then drove off back towards the zoo.

Unfortunately, on the way the van broke down so he had to stop and fiddle with the engine to try and get it started once again. This he did without success and started to get worried about the penguins because it was very hot in the back of the van.

So he was delighted when a few minutes later he saw a similar van driving over the hill. He stopped and flagged it down.

The zoo-keeper said to the man in the van: 'Please would you take my penguins to the zoo? My van has broken down and it's very uncomfortable for them in the back.'

The man replied that he would be very happy to take the penguins to the zoo. The keeper gave him £10 for his trouble and the man set off with the penguins safely in the back of his van.

The zoo-keeper was able to call the breakdown services, who quickly came and repaired his van, and soon he was back on his way to the zoo to see that the penguins had arrived safely.

Imagine his horror when he arrived at the zoo and found that there was no sign of the penguins at all. He jumped back in his van and drove off towards town to report the theft to the police, but as he was driving down the High Street who should he see but the van driver walking along the pavement with the penguins waddling along behind him.

The zoo-keeper was really angry and, winding down his window, shouted:

'Hey! What do you think you're doing? I gave you

£10 to take my penguins to the zoo!'

The man looked very distressed:

'I did take them to the zoo,' he cried, 'but there was some money left over, so now I'm taking them all to the cinema!'

The dustman called at a house to empty the bin and found that the occupier had overslept and forgotten to put it out. The dustman rang the bell and tapped on the door. After ten minutes an upstairs window opened and a sleepy head looked out.

'Where's yer bin?' asked the dustman.

'I bin asleep,' came the reply. 'Where's *you* bin?'

A man was driving down the middle of a country lane when suddenly his car stopped dead. He got out of the car and looked inside the bonnet to see if he could fix it.

Presently a cow ambled up beside him, took a look at the car and said, 'It's probably the carburettor.'

The man was so amazed that he ran down the road as fast as he could. Soon he saw a milkmaid walking towards him with two buckets of milk. He stopped her and told her exactly what had happened.

'Did the cow have a white patch in the middle of its forehead?' she asked.

'Yes, yes!' cried the motorist.

'Don't take any notice then. That know-all Dora, she don't know nothing about cars.'

Two mountain climbers had spent eight weeks climbing to the top of a mountain that had never been conquered before. It was an exhausting journey and they were near to collapse, but they struggled to the top. On reaching the summit one of the climbers turned to the other and said,

'It has almost cost us our lives to reach the top of this mountain, but it was worth it just to plant the British flag to show that we were here first. Hand me the flag.'

The other climber looked surprised and said, 'But I thought you brought it. . . .'

A father was anxious that his young son should grow out of the habit of gambling which he had developed, and he asked the boy's headmaster to help.

When the father called for the boy at the end of the term the headmaster said,

'I think I've cured your son of gambling.'

'How did you do that?' asked the father.

'Well, one day I saw him looking at my beard and he said: "Sir, is that a real beard or a false one? I wouldn't mind betting £5 that it's false."'

'All right,' I replied, 'I'll take your bet. Now pull it and see.'

'Of course, my beard is real so I made him pay me £5, and I'm sure I've cured him.'

'Oh dear,' groaned the father. 'He bet me £10 he would pull your beard before the end of term!'

Anybody can capture a crocodile. This is how you do it. First get a telescope, a matchbox, a pair of tweezers and a large, very boring book. Choose a steamy hot day and go down to the riverbank where crocodiles live. Just sit down with the telescope, matchbox and tweezers next to you and start to read. As it's a warm day and the book is dull and boring you will soon fall asleep.

After a while a crocodile is bound to see you and will come and investigate. He will peer over your shoulder and begin to read the boring book. Because the day is hot and the book is boring, he will soon fall asleep.

As soon as he does, you wake up. Pick up the telescope and look at the crocodile through the wrong end ... then, using your tweezers, pick him up, put him in the matchbox – and there you have your crocodile!

Looking the part

Being a joker and being funny doesn't only mean telling jokes, riddles or poems. You can look funny too! Visual humour can be just as hilarious as verbal jokes. Here's what you can do.

Clothes

Dressing up and putting on odd clothes is always fun, whether you are pretending to be somebody else, impersonating a famous character, going to fancy dress parties, or simply trying to fool your friends.

Start collecting old clothes and keep them in a box or suitcase. Visit jumble sales and fêtes where clothes are sold cheaply. Talk nicely to aunts and grandmas who might give you some clothes for nothing! Never refuse anything – you never know when it might come in useful!

Try dressing up as a little old lady or a tramp or an elegant gentleman, and see if you can disguise yourself so much that even your best friends do not recognise you. A good game for jokers is to get some friends to disguise themselves and then have a game seeing if people can guess who they really are. It is an excellent game for parties.

Wigs

By changing the colour and style of your hair you can make yourself look hilarious. Wigs can often be picked up very cheaply in secondhand clothes shops and charity shops, but you can easily make your own out of string or coloured wool.

Hats

A great deal of fun can be had by wearing funny hats. Look at some of the great comedians whose hats were so very important to their characters – Laurel and Hardy and Charlie Chaplin, with their bowler hats, Tommy Cooper with his fez, Frank Spencer's beret, and so on. Collect a variety of old hats and sit in front of a mirror trying them at ridiculous angles to see which looks the funniest.

Make-up

With just a few sticks of make-up you can greatly alter your appearance. From joke shops and theatrical costumiers you can buy sticks of make-up that real actors and comedians wear. The most commonly used are number 5 (Ivory) and number 9 (Brick red). You can build up your collection as you go along. To make yourself look really old, sit in front of a mirror and screw up your face as tightly as possible, then draw in the lines with an eyebrow pencil.

Practise your make-up carefully until you achieve the desired effect. With just a little practice you can easily turn yourself into a clown or a Red Indian, Count Dracula or a fairy-tale princess. Beards and moustaches can be made out of wool or string.

Remember, the most important part of your make-up is removing cream. It wouldn't be very funny if, having made yourself up to look like a clown, you couldn't get the paints off!'

Visual jokes

Finally, make the most of visual jokes. Trip over as you leave a room. Drop a parcel that you are carrying and catch it just before it reaches the ground. Open a bag of sweets and shoot them all over the table. Put an item of clothing on back to front.

Always be on the lookout for a funny situation and make the most of it, and you'll have them laughing in the aisles!

'They laughed when I sat down at the piano. I had forgotten to bring a stool!'

Silly walks

Practise silly walks as you go down the street or make your way to school! Swing each leg as far forward and as far backward as it will go and wave your arms up and down as you stride along.

Walk slowly with your knees bent and your feet 30 centimetres apart and you will look like somebody who is old.

Give yourself a limp by putting a pebble in one of your shoes. This will ensure that you remember to limp with the same foot all the time!

Padding

You can make yourself look really fat by putting cushions or pillows under your clothes. Your arms can be padded out by wrapping towels around them, and a towel worn around your shoulders underneath your costume will make you look very broad.

Funny faces

Funny faces always cause a laugh, whether it's sticking your tongue in your cheek or going cross-eyed. Take care that the wind doesn't change though, or you might stay like that!

Try this: Place your two index fingers in the corners of your mouth and pull them to give yourself a very wide grin. Now stick out your tongue as far as it will go, and try and look at the tip of your nose at the same time! The funny face you make will have your friends in stitches, but don't pull your mouth too hard, otherwise you'll need stitches too!

Knock, knock

Some jokes are guaranteed to knock you out! Simply say 'Knock, knock' and you'll discover that nobody can resist saying 'Who's there?' Try it and see! Here are some of the funniest knock, knock jokes around.

Knock, knock.
Who's there?
Luke.
Luke who?
Luke through the keyhole and you'll see.

Knock, knock.
Who's there?
Wendy.
Wendy who?
Wendy wed wed wobbing comes bob bob bobbin along ...

Knock, knock.
Who's there?
Felix.
Felix who?
Felix my lolly again I'll hit him.

Knock, knock.
Who's there?
Tank.
Tank who?
You're welcome.

Knock, knock.
Who's there?
The Avon lady. Your bell doesn't work.

Knock, knock.
Who's there?
Howard.
Howard who?
Howard you know if you don't open the door?

Knock, knock.
Who's there?
Isabelle.
Isabelle who?
Isabelle out of order? I had to knock.

Knock, knock.
Who's there?
Atch.
Atch who?
Bless you. I didn't know you'd got a cold.

Knock, knock.
Who's there?
Jemima.
Jemima who?
Jemima asking whose house this is?

Knock, knock.
Who's there?
Hurd.
Hurd who?
Hurd my hand knocking on this door.

Knock, knock.
Who's there?
Walter.
Walter who?
Walter wall carpets.

Knock, knock.
Who's there?
Shelby.
Shelby who?
Shelby coming round the mountain when she comes.

Knock, knock.
Who's there?
You.
You who?
You who! Is there anybody in?

Knock, knock.
Who's there?
Buster.
Buster who?
Buster the cemetery gates, please.

Knock, knock.
Who's there?
Sari.
Sari who?
Sari, I was sarong.

Knock, knock.
Who's there?
Rabbit.
Rabbit who?
Rabbit up nicely. It's a present.

Knock, knock.
Who's there?
Sam and Janet.
Sam and Janet who?
Sam and Janet evening, you may see a stranger . . .

Knock, knock.
Who's there?
Zookeeper.
Zookeeper who?
Zookeeper way from me if you've got germs.

Knock, knock.
Who's there?
Fanny.
Fanny who?
Fannybody home?

Knock, knock.
Who's there?
Miniature.
Miniature who?
Miniature open your mouth, you put your foot in it.

Knock, knock.
Who's there?
Thumb.
Thumb who?
Thumb like it hot, thumb like it cold.

Knock, knock.
Who's there?
Sonia.
Sonia who?
Sonia foot. I can smell it from here.

Knock, knock.
Who's there?
Sybil.
Sybil who?
Sybil Simon met a pieman . . .

Knock, knock.
Who's there?
Tyrone.
Tyrone who?
Tyrone shoe laces. You're big enough now.

Knock, knock.
Who's there?
Freddie.
Freddie who?
Freddie or not, here I come.

Knock, knock.
Who's there?
Shirley.
Shirley who?
Shirley you must know by now.

Knock, knock.
Who's there?
Jester.
Jester who?
Jester song at twilight.

Knock, knock.
Who's there?
Eileen.
Eileen who?
Eileen'd on your fence and broke it.

93

Knock, knock.
Who's there?
Gestapo.
Gestapo who?
Ve ask the questions!

Knock, knock.
Who's there?
Ya.
Ya who?
Never knew you were a cowboy.

Knock, knock.
Who's there?
Chilly.
Chilly who?
Chilly me, I've forgotten.

Knock, knock.
Who's there?
Closure.
Closure who?
Closure mouth while you're eating.

Knock, knock.
Who's there?
Yelp.
Yelp who?
Yelp me! I've got my nose stuck in the keyhole.

Knock, knock.
Who's there?
Matthew.
Matthew who?
Matthew laces came undone.

Knock, knock.
Who's there?
Cynthia.
Cynthia who?
Cynthia been away, I've been blue.

Knock, knock.
Who's there?
Thumping.
Thumping who?
Thumping green and slimy is climbing up your neck.

Knock, knock.
Who's there?
Boo.
Boo who?
Just boo. I'm a ghost.

Knock, knock.
Who's there?
Bernadette.
Bernadette who?
Bernadette all my dinner.

Knock, knock.
Who's there?
Althea.
Althea who?
Althea later.

Knock, knock.
Who's there?
Oscar.
Oscar who?
Oscar silly question, you get a silly answer.

Knock, knock.
Who's there?
Alex.
Alex who?
Alex the questions if you don't mind.

Knock, knock.
Who's there?
Danielle.
Danielle who?
Danielle so loud! We can hear you.

Knock, knock.
Who's there?
Hosanna.
Hosanna who?
Hosanna Claus gets down the chimney, I'll never know.

Knock, knock.
Who's there?
Howell.
Howell who?
Howell you know unless you open the door?

Knock, knock.
Who's there?
Harvey.
Harvey who?
Harvey going to play this game forever?

Knock, knock.
Who's there?
Sophie.
Sophie who?
Sophie are going to stop telling knock, knock jokes.

Knock, knock.
Who's there?
Zsa Zsa.
Zsa Zsa who?
Zsa Zsa last knock, knock joke I want to hear!!

Knock, knock.
Who's there?
Gus.
Gus who?
Gus what we're going to do now.

Jester minute

There have always been jokers. Ever since man first set foot on the earth, he's been falling flat on his face in the mud, which is probably why man is the only animal in the world that can laugh. He's also the only animal that blushes – or needs to!

Although we can never be certain, I suspect that cavemen were jokers. They thought it was great fun to hit each other over the head with a large club, and no doubt served hollow dinosaur eggs just for a laugh, and probably hid prehistoric monsters in dark corners of their caves just to scare the wife.

Five thousand years ago in Ancient Egypt, the powerful Pharaohs had jokers in their palaces to entertain them. These jokers were known as *dangas* and were the very first court jesters. When a Pharaoh grew tired of building pyramids, or having people thrown into the Nile, he would send for his *danga* to entertain him, presumably with Egyptian jokes.

What did Mark Anthony say to Cleopatra when she started to look tired?

'Why don't you snake it easy!'

In Ancient Rome it is said that entertainment was controlled by the Goddess Thalia, the Muse of Comedy, probably the Queen of the Jokers, and a statue of her can be seen in the Vatican. She is holding a comic mask and a tambourine, so she obviously enjoyed a bit of fun! She was assisted by little creatures known as Fauns and Satyrs, and today if we write a little poem or composition in which we make someone look a fool and ridicule them, it is called a 'satire'.

Later, in England, kings from Richard the Lionheart onwards had Court Jesters to keep them amused. Henry VIII and even Elizabeth I had them. This was an age when television was unheard of, there were very few theatres, certainly not as we know them today, and people couldn't go and watch a film or go out for a ride in a car. So they needed other means of entertainment, and this came in the form of a jester.

Jesters were looked upon as fools and knaves, but actually a jester needed to be a very clever person and very funny too, otherwise he lost his head! A jester had to be able to tell jokes (usually about the king himself and members of the court; the jester being the only person in the land who was allowed to make fun of the monarch) tell funny stories, do acrobatics, juggle, dance, sing – in fact anything the king or queen commanded. The jester could be called to perform at any time of the day or night, whether he felt like telling jokes or not. In medieval times jesters wore a special costume too – a hat that had three points on it and a bell hanging from each – so that this comical figure looked ridiculous and could be easily recognised.

By 1600 clowns were becoming popular. The most famous troupe was known as Commedia dell'Arte – a group of clowns who travelled around Italy doing slapstick, telling jokes and performing comic stunts very much as clowns in a circus do today. Often the comedy routines that clowns perform are handed down from generation to generation and have changed very little over the years. It was at this time that clowns started to wear funny make-up, and the Pierrot or white-faced clown made his first appearance.

Just like today's circuses, these clowns travelled all over Europe, performing on village greens and market squares, but it was not until two hundred years ago that the red-nosed clown with the baggy suit, that we all know and love, made his first appearance.

It all happened quite by accident when a particular clown got into serious trouble, and decided to run away from the circus in Germany. In order that the circus manager should not recognise him he tried to disguise himself by putting on a red wig and a suit that was much too large for him. Suddenly, he spotted the manager, and in a bid to get away from him, jumped through a hole in the tent and landed slap bang in the middle of the arena. Every time he tried to stand up . . . whoops! He fell flat on his back!

The audience loved it, thinking it was all part of the act, and shouted 'Auguste!' which is German for 'Clumsy Fool!' The circus manager liked it too, and so the clown had a job for life and no longer needed to run away. Even today, the baggy-suited clown who always falls over, and gets covered in custard pies and whitewash, is known as the 'Auguste Clown'.

By the end of the eighteenth century a new era for jokers began. This was a mixture of jesters and clowns and Greek and Roman satires, and is something we still enjoy today – pantomime. Pantomimes are always packed full of men dressed as women, women dressed as men and people dressed as animals, there is circus-like slapstick, old jokes and new jokes – real family entertainment that is a must for every joker.

Within a few years the Music Hall developed. Music Halls were theatres where variety shows were performed, consisting of singing, dancing, comic sketches, and always a comedian telling jokes. Music Halls remained popular until the early part of this century, when the silent comedy films introduced new jokers to the world – Buster Keaton, Laurel and Hardy and that lovable little tramp, Charlie Chaplin, who really stole the limelight.

With the development of television and radio as popular forms of entertainment, comedians and jokers as we know them today began to entertain. We don't know what will happen next in the world, but one thing is certain – all the world loves a joker and old jokes never die . . . they're simply told over and over again!

Insulting behaviour

I wish I had your picture.
It would be very nice.
I'd hang it in the cellar
To scare away the mice!

A joker must never cause offence or hurt anyone's feelings, but make people laugh and you can insult them without their even realising it! Here's a selection of the funniest insults and most hilarious put-downs you can ever hurl at anybody . . .

'Is that your real face or are you wearing a gas mask?'

'My brother was born upside-down. His nose runs and his feet smell.'

'Don't look out of the window – people will think it's Hallowe'en.'

'I have a hunch.'
'And here was me thinking you were round-shouldered.'

'I never forget a face, but in your case I'll make an exception.'

'My sister must be twenty-five. I counted the rings under her eyes.'

'She looks like she just stepped out of a beauty parlour – and then fell flat on her face.'

'Her tongue is so long, she can lick an envelope after she's posted it.'

'You're not yourself today? Thank goodness!'

'Please close your mouth, I'd like to see the rest of your face.'

'He has muscles in his arms like potatoes – mashed potatoes.'

'I like your dress, but aren't you a bit early for Hallowe'en?'

The rain makes all things beautiful,
The trees and flowers too.
If rain makes all things beautiful,
Why doesn't it rain on you?

'You've got a good singing voice – if you don't happen to like music.'

'I haven't shown you my holiday photos.'
'No, and I appreciate it.'

'You're much cleverer than you look, but then I suppose you'd have to be.'

'That's a nice dress you're wearing. Pity they didn't have it in your size.'

'Please shut your mouth. There's a terrible draught in here.'
'I've got a minute to spare – tell me everything you know.'

'What vanity! He goes into the garden so that flowers can smell him.'

'Don't go to a mind-reader, go to a palmist. At least you've got a palm.'

'Beauty isn't everything. In your case it's nothing.'

'They call her "Dressmaker" because she's always making slips.'

'You look a million – every single year of it.'

'She's got long black hair running down her back. Pity it's not on her head.'

'He went to a mind-reader the other day and was charged half price.'

'He's watched so many detective stories on television, when he turns off the set he wipes his fingerprints off the knob.'

'I call him "Laryngitis" because he's a pain in the neck.'

'She's got a heart of gold – yellow and hard.'

'I thought he always wore black gloves until he washed his hands.'

Roses are red,
Violets are blue.
Umbrellas get lost,
So why don't you?

'I'd like to help you out – which way did you come in?'

'There's nothing wrong with your brain. Nothing that a transplant wouldn't cure.'

'If you don't say you love me I'll blow my brains out.'
'Go on, then. You've got nothing to lose.'

'I wish I had ten pence for every boy that has askd me to marry him.'
'What would you buy – a packet of peppermints?'

'Of course I enjoy your cooking. Do you have a stomach pump handy?'

'Is that your face or are you breaking it in for a baboon?'

'If I give you a scale, will you go weigh?'

> I wish I were a dozen eggs
> Balanced above your bed,
> And when you went to lie on it,
> I'd smash right on your head!
>
> I wish I were a grapefruit,
> And here's the reason why.
> When you came to eat me,
> I'd squirt juice right in your eye!

'Is it true that you were such a rotten child, your parents ran away from home.'

'You sound so much better with your mouth closed.'

'She's so unpopular, even the telephone doesn't ring when she's in the bath.'

'Am I pretty as a picture?'
'Yes, but your frame is in a mess.'

'She has such beautiful hair. Every time we go out I insist that she wears it.'

'You have a wonderful head on your shoulders. Whose is it?'

'That suit fits you like a glove – it sticks out in five places.'

'The last time I saw a face like yours I threw it a fish.'

'Everytime it rains
I think of you:
Drip . . . drip . . . drip . . .'

'When I look at you, time stands still. Your face would stop any clock.'

'Do you think I should let my hair grow?'
'Yes. Right over your face.'

'Sorry, my mind was wandering.'
'Don't worry – it's too weak to go very far.'

'When I was born they fired a twenty-one gun salute.'
'Pity they missed.'

'I could go on dancing like this forever.'
'Don't you ever want to improve.'

'His hair is so wavy, I get seasick just looking at it.'

106

'I'd like to tell you how I feel about you, but not while I'm eating.'

'I like the way you dress. Who wears your clean clothes?'

'You'd make a perfect stranger!'

'Now, if you have somewhere to go – go!'

Howlers

Did you know that every day, all over the world, hundreds of children are being jokers *without even realising it*? Yes, I have visited schools throughout the United Kingdom, the United States of America, Australia and many other English-speaking countries and have looked into exercise books *just like yours*! As a result, I have gathered together one hundred of the worst – and whackiest – genuine howlers, bloomers and blunders.

1. A centimetre is an insect with a hundred legs.

2. Margarine is made from imitation cows.

3. A blizzard is the inside of a chicken.

4. The second wife of Henry VIII was Anne Berlin.

5. Magnets are little creatures that eat rotten apples.

6. Alligator shoes are made from crocodile skins.

7. The smallest wind instrument is the Piccadilly.

8. Moths eat hardly nothing, except holes.

9. Florence Nightingale was a famous Swedish soprano.

10. The Pope lives in the Vacuum.

11. Tunisia is a disease where you lose your memory.

12. A spatula is the bone that holds up your shoulder blade.

13. Jacob had a brother called See-Saw.

14. A parole is a special kind of bun they eat in prisons.

15. Livid was a famous Roman poet.

16. A plumber is a man who picks plums for a living.

17. Macaroni invented the radio.

18. Vandals are open-toed shoes worn by the Romans.

19. A goatee is a miniature goat.

20. People who test your eyes are called optimists.

21. A hostage is a nice lady on an aeroplane.

22. Handel was a small boy in a fairy tale by Grimm who had a sister called Gristle.

23. Venison is a city in Italy with lots of canals.

24. A centurion is a Roman who is a hundred years old.

25. An oxygen has eight sides.

26. I had salad for launch today.

27. A medicine ball is a dance for sick people.

28. The sewage canal is in Egypt.

29. Monsoon is the French word for Mister.

30. Cleopatra died from the bite of a wasp.

31. Conservation is when you talk to people.

32. Eli Whitney was a barman who invented a drink called cotton gin.

33. Ancient Tyre was the wheel of a Roman chariot.

34. Bamboo was a little fawn in a Disney cartoon.

35. Pegasus is a hobby horse used by carpenters.

36. 'Dieu et mon droit' means 'My God, and you're right.'

37. 'Non, je ne regrette rien' means 'I don't mind if I do.'

38. 'Debate' is something you hang on your hook when you go fishing.

39. The bowels are a, e, i, o and u.

40. There are a lot of currants in the sea.

41. A fjord is a Norwegian car.

42. At the coronation the Queen carried an orb and spectre.

43. A woman who has many husbands is called a pollyanna.

44. 'Coup' is French for chicken house.

45. Taxes is a place with a lot of cowboys.

46. Anatomy is something we all have but looks better on girls.

47. A cortege is a small country house.

48. Writers are very strange because teacher says tails come out of their heads.

49. The 'Amazon' is something very surprising.

50. A hippie is a tiny little hippo.

51. Noah's wife was Joan of Arc.

52. 'The lady smiled at him displacing a beautiful set of white teeth.'

53. Ladies who sing two sorts of song are called contralto.

54. If you get hit on the head the insurance pays you a lump sum.

55. A hangnail is what you bang in the wall to hang a picture on.

56. The British Isles has a temporary climate.

57. Polonius was a sort of sausage.

58. Henry VIII had an abbess on each knee and could not walk.

59. A Russian is a man who sits on nothing and dances.

60. A silverfish is an imitation goldfish.

61. An aviary is a place where aviators sleep.

62. A palmist is someone who tells your fortune by looking in a crystal ball.

63. A monk is a chimp who wears a habit.

64. A refugee is a man who takes charge at a football match.

65. An elephant is an animal with a vacuum cleaner in front.

66. Hydrogin is a chemical made from water and gin.

67. Chivalry is the action of a man to a strange woman.

68. Etching is when a dog has fleas.

69. 'Census' is sight, sound and touch.

70. The earth resolves around the sun once a year.

71. Herrings swim about the sea wearing shawls.

72. A leaflet is a small leaf.

73. The Congo is a dance when you get in a long line.

74. Good manners is the noise you don't make when you eat your soup.

75. Marseillaise is a French salad dressing.

76. Quadrupeds has no singular. You can't have a horse with one leg.

77. A fencer is a man who puts up fences.

78. A marionette is a net which you catch marions in.

79. A wombat is what you use to play a game of wom.

80. Letters in sloping type are called hysterics.

81. A flying buttress is a lady buttress on an aeroplane.

82. There was a fowl smell in the chicken hut.

83. Sienna is an Italian city famous for being burnt.

84. Electric vaults are named after Voltaire who invented electricity.

85. Kosher is Jewish pork.

86. A connoisseur is a man who opens taxi doors outside posh hotels.

87. There are four symptoms of a cold. Two I forget and the other two are well known.

88. How do you spell 'hair' when you mean rabbit?

89. A surname is the name of somebody you say 'Sir' to.

90. Pelicans are expensive to feed because of their large bills.

91. In some games of golf you have to play a handy cup.

92. Mata Hari means suicide in Japan.

93. A surefooted animal is an animal that when it kicks is sure it will not miss.

94. A trapezium is what they swing on in a circus.

95. Lumbago is a mineral that they make pencils out of.

96. A criminal is someone who gets caught.

97. *Agape* is French for a big hole.

98. A cuckoo is a bird which lays other birds' eggs in its nest.

99. Chlorine gas is very dangerous to humans so it should be an experiment only performed on the teacher.

100. *Aperitif* is French for dentures.

Good book guide

Have you ever read *Over the Cliff* by Eileen Dover, or *Crossing the Desert* by Rhoda Camel? If not, here's a list of best-selling books that you must look out for. Why not give it to your teacher and see if any of the titles are in your school library?

Ten Years in the Ape House *by Bab Boone*
Come On In *by Maud D. Merrier*
I Love Toffees *by Oliver Nutherone*
The Dangerous Lion *by Claudia Armoff*
Five Babies *by Bertha Quinns*
Time for School *by R. U. Upjohn*
Hair Care *by Dan Druff*
The Housing Problem *by Rufus Quick*
Improve Your Target Shooting *by Mr Completely*
A Matter of Doubt *by Willie Wontie*
Banbury Cross *by Rhoda Whitehorse*
The Work of a Policeman *by Laura Norder*
The Story of a Highwayman *by Ann Dover*
I'll Pour You a Drink *by Bart Ender*
Sad Woman *by Paul Aidy*
Get Rich Quick *by Robin Banks*
Collecting Old Furniture *by Ann Teak*
The Welsh Comedian *by Dai Larfin*
Tug of War *by Paul Hard*
Hole in My Bucket *by Lee King*
It's a Hold Up *by Nick R. Elastic*
Which Way Out? *by Isadora Neggsitt*

Hole in My Bucket *by Lee King*
It's Impossible *by Freda Carnt*
How to Pray *by Neil Down*
The Tale of a Vandal *by Eva Brick*
Is It Love? *by Midas Wellbe*
How to Avoid Arguments *by Xavier Breath*
In the Countryside *by Theresa Greene*
The Short Snack *by T. N. Biscuits*
Warming up the Room *by Ray D. Aitor*
Against the Law *by Kermit A. Crime*
The Unemployed Conjurer *by Trixie Coulden-Doo*
Born First *by Imelda Thanyou*
The Suburbs *by Bill Tupparea*
Deep Sleep *by Annie Sthetic*
The Haunted House *by Hugo First*
Detective Stories *by Watts E. Dunn*

Christmas Decorations *by Holly Branch and Miss L. Toe*

Who Saw Him Leave? *by Wendy Go*

Certainty *by R. U. Shaw*

The Match on the Grass *by Lorna Light*

Someone Else's Trousers *by Titus Canbe*

The Great Escape *by Freda Convict*

Hide and Seek *by I. C. Hugh*

Off to Market *by Tobias A. Pigg*

1066 *by Norman Invasion*

I Want to See You *by Tamara Knight*

The Winner *by Vic Tree*

The Ugly Hag *by Ida Face*

The Naughty Schoolboy *by Enid Spanking*

School Dinners *by R. E. Volting*

How to Get There *by Ridya Bike*

A Close Shave *by Aaron Floor*

How to Apologise *by Thayer Thorry*

How to Feed Elephants *by P. Nutts*

Aches and Pains *by Arthur Ritis*

The Spicy Sausage *by Della Katesen*

The Flower Garden *by Polly Anthus*

Hit on the Head *by I. C. Starrs*

Never Give Up *by Percy Vere*

The Calypso Band *by Lydia Dustbin*

Looking Forward *by Felix Ited*

The Electric Drill *by Andy Gadgett*

Fifty Metres to the Bus Stop *by Willy Makitt, illustrated by Betty Wont*

Round the Mountain *by Sheila B. Cummin*

Economic Breakfast *by Roland Marge*

Keeping Cheerful *by Mona Lott*

The Post Script *by Adeline Extra*

Family fun

It doesn't have to be April Fool's Day for you to play practical jokes. You can make fools of your family any day of the year! Here's a joke to play on each member of the family in turn.

Mother

Have you noticed how mothers have a habit of sending you up to bed at exactly the time the best programme on television starts?

'Come on! It's time for you to go to bed . . .'

Have you noticed how, when you're playing your favourite game, and you are just about to win . . .

'Come on! It's school tomorrow. Now get to bed.'

Have you noticed that it is always when you feel really wide awake and quite able to stay up for hours and hours in the evening that Mother's voice echoes around the room . . .

'You'll never be up in the morning!'

To show mother how foolish she is, simply put the clocks back! About an hour before your usual bedtime, sneak around the house and put all the clocks back about two hours and don't say a word to anybody. Eventually your mother will say those magic words: 'Come on! It's bedtime!' to which you reply: 'Aw! Mum! It's only six o'clock!'

Naturally she will go and have a look at the clock to make sure. She may even go and have a look at more

118

than one clock, and she will see that you are right. You can even offer to telephone the speaking clock for her, which you will do just to confirm that the time really is only six o'clock.

Sooner or later your mother will realise that it is all a practical joke, but at least it will enable you to stay up much later than usual!

Father

When fathers go to bed they usually wear pyjamas. Often enormous creations that make them look much more like clowns! Well, why not make a clown out of your father tonight. At some time during the day, go into his bedroom and find out where his pyjamas are kept. They may be under the pillow, on a chair, or where he stepped out of them on the floor!

Take the pyjama trousers and turn them inside-out. Tie a knot in one of the legs near the ankle, and turn them back the correct way again. Now put the pyjamas back exactly where you found them so that he will have no idea that anyone has touched them.

That night when he goes to put his pyjamas on, he will put one leg in as normal, but for some reason his other leg just won't seem to go in however hard he pushes! Only you know the reason why. But it can't possibly be anything to do with you – after all, you're tucked up fast asleep in bed!

Brother

While your father is struggling to get into his pyjamas, you might as well make it a night of fun by playing a trick on your brother while he is in bed too!

For this joke you will need a tin tray, an empty yoghurt pot, and some dried peas. Fill the pot with the peas, and just before your brother goes to bed, pour some hot water on them. Stand the pot on the metal tray and hide them on top of his wardrobe where he can't see them.

As the water begins to soak into the peas they will expand and start pushing the dried peas at the top over the edge so that they land on the tin tray making a very spooky sound. Could it be that your brother has a ghost in his room? Tell him a ghost story before he goes to bed and it will be even more frightening!

Experiment with this joke first. You may find that if the tray is raised up just a little, perhaps with a matchbox under each corner, you will get a better sound. It might help to stand the yoghurt pot on something too, as the further the peas have to fall, the louder and more frightening the sound will be.

Sister

While big brother is trying to work out where the ghostly noises are coming from, you could give your sister a few surprises too!

For her you will need some little bells. The kind that hang in budgie cages are ideal, and can be bought for only a few pence from any pet shop. You can get quite a large number very cheaply.

Using some pieces of cotton or string, tie them to the springs underneath your sister's bed where they cannot be seen. Unless she happens to go under her bed for anything, which is unlikely, she will not notice them until she gets into bed. Then every time she moves in bed she will hear a strange tinkling sound. Naturally, every time she hears this sound she will lie very still trying hard to hear where it is coming from, but of course it will only happen when she moves.

Grandma

It's no good playing practical jokes on your grandmother when she's in bed. Once the hearing aid is turned off, she won't notice anything!

Grandmas, however, *always* have large sensible umbrellas, which they carry everywhere with them just in case it rains. The next time Grandma visits you, you can play a practical joke on her using her umbrella.

When nobody is looking, open the umbrella out a little and pour some confetti inside. Little shreads of newspaper will do if you don't have any confetti or coloured paper. Close the umbrella up tightly once again, and nobody will know that it is any different from normal.

Grandma, of course, will not open the umbrella until it actually rains, which could be several days or even weeks later, but when she does – which could be in the middle of the High Street, or whilst walking out of church with the vicar – whooosh! she will be showered, not with rain, but with confetti!

Grandpa

Just as Grandmas always have umbrellas, Grandpas always have their head in a newspaper. There is nothing they like better!

The next time you are visiting your grandpa, or when he is next staying with you, try and get to the morning paper before he has a chance to see it. Take off the front pages and hide the inside ones carefully where they will not be found, but will not be accidentally destroyed either.

Take the middle pages from an old newspaper and put them inside the covers of the new newspaper. Leave the paper lying around and eventually grandpa will pick it up and begin to read it. Sit very quietly and watch him, and see just how long it is before he notices that the news he is reading is last week's!

Another joke that is much more fun but takes time to prepare is to take the middle pages from an old newspaper and glue them all together. Place this inside the cover of today's newspaper and wait. When Grandpa picks up the paper he will wonder why he can't open the inside pages!

Warning: Never glue together the pages of today's paper before anybody has read it. Otherwise *you* might come to a sticky end!

Everybody's laughing

Just recently I carried out a survey to see just what makes everybody laugh, and I discovered some pretty amazing things! For instance, do you know what kind of joke makes people laugh more than anything in the world? It's the ... No! I'm not going to tell you! You can find out for yourself!

Here's a little survey that you can do for yourself amongst your friends, or you can even stop people in the street and see if they can complete the following questionnaire.

1 Here are three different versions of the same joke. Only one is correct. Circle the number of the joke that is told correctly.

a *What do you call a bad-tempered tiger with cotton wool in his ears?*
'What?'
'I don't know.'

b *What do you call a bad-tempered tiger with cotton wool in his ears?*
'What?'
'Nothing. What's snoo with you?'

c *What do you call a bad-tempered tiger with cotton wool in his ears?*
'What?'
'Anything you like. He can't hear you!'

2 Complete the following two knock, knock jokes:

Knock, knock.
Who's there?
Turnips.
Turnips who?

. . . .

Knock, knock.
Who's there?
Oscar.
Oscar who?

. . . .

3 Good jokers know the punchlines to every joke. Here's a list of jokes and a list of punchlines. Can you match them up?

1 Why do giraffes have long necks?

a To hold their trousers up.

2 Why did the man pull a piece of string?

b Because fleas can't have elephants.

3 How do you hire a horse?

c He'd look silly pushing it.

4 What do you call a postman with eight children?

d Because their feet smell.

5 Why did the elephant have fleas?

e Stand it on four bricks.

6 What goes 99-clop?

f Frostbite.

7 What do you get if you cross a snowman with Jaws?

g A centipede with a wooden leg.

8 Why do sailors have red, white and blue braces?

h Daddy.

4 What would make you laugh the most?

a Your teacher slipping on a banana skin.
b Grandma stepping on her glasses.
c Your best friend bending over and ripping his
   trousers.
d Taking a drink from the water fountain and
   spurting people halfway down the road.
e Getting a custard pie in your face.

5 What is the funniest thing you could do with a
   plate of cold tripe?

6 You are sitting at the dinner table with Dermot,
   Wendy, Sarah and Joachim.
      Joachim puts a poached egg on each eye and
   says: 'Do you think I need glasses?'
      Wendy butters her serviette and says: 'They
   don't make white bread like they used to.'
      Sarah spills milk all over you and says: 'Don't
   cry over spilt milk.'
      Dermot puts a fork in his roast beef, goes
   'Moooo' and says: 'I think this is still alive.'
      Who would make you laugh the most?

7 Here are five 'Doctor' jokes. Which would you say
   was the funniest?

   DOCTOR: *What seems to be the trouble?*
   PATIENT: I keep thinking that when I speak no one
      can hear me.
   DOCTOR: *What seems to be the trouble?*

   PATIENT: *I keep thinking there are two of me.*
   DOCTOR: Will you repeat that, and this time don't
      both speak at the same time.

125

WOMAN: *I'm worried about my husband. For the last year he's thought that he's a chicken.*

DOCTOR: Why haven't you been to see me before?

WOMAN: *I would have, but we couldn't do without the eggs.*

PATIENT: *The trouble is I can't stop pulling ugly faces.*

DOCTOR: That's not a serious problem.

PATIENT: *But people with ugly faces don't like it when I pull them.*

PATIENT: *Doctor, I'm scared to death of birds. When I see even a tiny sparrow I break out into a cold sweat.*

DOCTOR: But why are you afraid of birds?

PATIENT: *Aren't most worms?*

8 Do you find any of these funny?

a Kissing aunties.

b Staying in after school to write out 200 lines saying: 'I must not laugh at Miss Potts when the blackboard falls off the wall and hits her on the head.'

c Eating a plateful of cold cabbage.

d Having measles during the school holidays.

e Arriving in fancy dress at a party, only to discover nobody else is in fancy dress.

9 Which is the correct answer to the joke question: *'What did one rock pool say to the other rock pool?'*

a 'Show us your mussels.'

b 'There is not mushroom here.'

c 'Anything you like – he'll never hear you.'

10 Can you complete the missing parts in each of these jokes?

a '. . . . .'
   'I don't know, but there's one crawling up your neck.'

b 'How do you stop a . . . .?'
   'Eat it the night before.'

c 'What do you do with a sick kangaroo?'
   '. . . . .'

Get as many people as you can to take part in this silly survey and see what results come up. Keep a note of all the answers you are given and you'll find that you're in for a laugh – you might even discover some new jokes. Finally, at the end of the survey ask questions 11 and 12:

11 What makes you laugh the most?

12 What is the funniest joke you have ever heard?

Double trouble

If you have an accomplice or fellow joker, you can have double the amount of fun by trying the following:

Playing tricks

At a party you and your friend stand on either side of a box or low stool and get your victim to stand on it. You then blindfold your victim so that he or she cannot see anything, and get him to rest one hand on your shoulder and one on your friend's shoulder.

You then announce that you are going to lift the box high into the air. Both you and your friend kneel on the floor at the same time. You haven't touched the box, but the victim standing there blindfolded will get the impression that you have lifted him into the air. You then say: 'Right. Now we would like you to jump to the floor.'

Of course, he will not dare do this because it seems such a very long way down. You then remove the blindfold and show your victim that the box hasn't moved an inch. It's a simple trick but always very effective.

Practical jokes

You and your friend stand in the middle of a busy pavement and one of you points up towards the sky or the top of a building. Just stand there looking up and it will not be long before you are joined by a large crowd of people gazing into the air. You both then walk away, and you will leave a group of very puzzled people behind, wondering exactly what they are looking at.

Ventriloquism

With the help of a friend you can become a ventriloquist in just a few minutes. That is because you cheat! You can sit on a table with your doll or dummy on your knee and have a conversation with it. Nobody will see your lips move when the dummy speaks. That is because they won't move! Your friend will be hidden under the table where nobody can see him, and *he* can be the dummy's voice. You can work out a very funny script beforehand, and soon you will be hailed as the world's greatest ventriloquist – as long as your friend keeps out of sight!

Alternatively, you can have fun by getting your friend to be the dummy. Dress him up like a schoolboy with short trousers and a school cap. With a used matchstick you can draw two lines down either side of his mouth from the corner of his lips going down to his chin so that it looks like a wooden dummy, and with a spot of lipstick you can give him two rosy cheeks. Sit your 'dummy' on your knee like a proper ventriloquist's dummy and you are ready to entertain!

Telling jokes

Sit on a bus and have funny conversations by speaking in jokes. Watch the reactions of your fellow passengers!

'I've taken up horse riding.'
'How are you getting on?'
'Somebody gives me a leg up. But it's more off than on.'
'You should take a running jump. Is it a good horse?'
'Oh yes, he's very polite.'
'Polite? A horse?'
'Yes. Whenever we jump a fence, he always lets me go first.'
'I hear you've just come back from India.'
'Yes, I was the guest of a rajah.'
'Really? Did you go hunting?'
'Oh yes. One day we went to the jungle to shoot tigers.'
'Any luck?'
'Yes. We didn't meet any!'

Crazy signs

As you travel around look out for some of these signs of the times. Outside a restaurant in New York recently I saw a sign that said:

> OUR CUTLERY IS NOT MEDICINE
> AND SHOULD NOT
> BE TAKEN AFTER MEALS

Sign in a cemetery:
PEOPLE ARE FORBIDDEN TO PICK FLOWERS
FROM ANY GRAVE OTHER THAN THEIR OWN

Sign in a dry-cleaner's:
CUSTOMERS WHO HAVE LEFT GARMENTS
LONGER THAN 30 DAYS WILL BE DISPOSED OF

Sign outside a pet shop:
NO DOGS ALLOWED

Sign in street:
NO WAITING AT ANY TIME.
PLEASE QUEUE HERE.

Sign in butcher's shop:
PORK FROM PIGS THAT DIED HAPPY

Sign in department store:
LIFT OUT OF ORDER. PLEASE USE ELEVATOR.

Sign in a classroom:
LAUGH AND THE CLASS LAUGHS WITH YOU,
BUT YOU STAY AFTER SCHOOL ALONE

131

Sign in a department store:
LIFT OUT OF ORDER. PLEASE USE ELEVATOR

Sign outside a dress shop:
DON'T STAND OUTSIDE AND FAINT
– COME INSIDE AND HAVE A FIT!

Sign in hen house:
THERE'S NOTHING DISGRACEFUL IN BEING
CHICKEN

Sign in department store:
BARGAIN BASEMENT UPSTAIRS

Sign in a garage:
DO NOT SMOKE.
EVEN IF YOUR LIFE ISN'T WORTH ANYTHING,
PETROL IS!

Sign in theatre:

SHAKESPEARE MARRIED AN AVON LADY

Sign in pet shop:

WET PETS!

Sign outside hairdresser's:

WE CURL UP AND DYE FOR YOU

also:

EARS PIERCED WHILE YOU WAIT

Sign in street:

AVOID THAT RUNDOWN FEELING
– LOOK BOTH WAYS BEFORE YOU CROSS

Sign on a lawn:

YOUR FEET ARE KILLING ME

Sign outside a dry cleaner's:
IF YOUR CLOTHES AREN'T BECOMING TO YOU
THEY SHOULD BE COMING TO US

Sign outside a doctor's surgery:
AN APPLE A DAY IS BAD FOR BUSINESS

Sign in King Arthur's court:
SIGN UP NOW FOR KNIGHT SCHOOL

Best of the bunch

Since I have been writing joke books, hundreds of jokers everywhere have kindly sent me their favourite jokes. Here are fifty of the best!

50. TEACHER: *What's garlic, Lillie?*
    LILLIE: It's a sort of language that Scotsmen speak.

49. ARTHUR: *You said your mother was dying, but I've just seen her come out of the hairdresser's.*
    MONICA: Yes. She's got a job there colouring people's hair.

48. *Where did Noah keep his bees?*
    In archives.

47. '*There were three elephants in a field – Fatima, Nelly and What. Fatima and Nelly decided to go for a walk. Who was left?*'
    'What?'
    '*There were three elephants in a field . . .*'

46. TOURIST GUIDE: *That brass plaque on the deck is where Nelson died.*
    TOURIST: I'm not surprised, I nearly tripped over it myself.

45. *'My brother's been practising the violin for twenty years.'*
'He must be good by now.'
'Not really. It was nineteen years before he realised you weren't supposed to blow it.'

44. *'Did the butcher have pig's feet, Winifred?'*
'I couldn't see, Mum. He had his shoes on.'

43. My gran is 82 years old and hasn't a grey hair on her head.
She's bald.

42. *What do you call a rabbit with a lot of money?*
A million hare.

41. MOTHER: *If you've finished your meal you can say grace.*
WILLIAM: O.K. Thanks for the meal, Lord.
MOTHER: *That wasn't much of a grace.*
WILLIAM: It wasn't much of a meal.

40. In a railway carriage a little boy kept sniffing.
'Haven't you got a handkerchief?' asked an old lady sitting opposite.
'Yes,' said the boy, 'but I don't think Mum would like me lending it to strangers.'

39. OPTICIAN: *Can you read the chart on the wall?*
PATIENT: What wall?

38. *How can you tell an elephant from a banana?*
Pick it up. If you can't, it's either an elephant or a very heavy banana.

37. *'Did the mudpack help your wife's appearance?'*
'It did, but it fell off after a few days.'

36. *'That last grapefruit was terrible.'*
'Just wait until you get an eyeful of this one.'

136

35. GUEST: *Didn't you say this boarding house was only a stone's throw from the sea?*
    LANDLADY: Yes, keep practising. You'll soon be able to throw a stone two miles.

34. *'I don't know whether to be a poet or a painter.'*
    'A poet!'
    'Oh, you've read one of my poems?'
    'No, I've seen one of your paintings.'

33. *What did one candle say to the other candle?*
    'Are you going out tonight?'

32. *'My teacher does bird impressions.'*
    'Really?'
    'Yes, she watches me like a hawk.'

31. *Why did the little boy eat a brick?*
    To build himself up.

30. *What is Father Christmas's wife's name?*
    Mary Christmas.

29. *'Mum, am I made of sage and onion?'*
    'Of course not. Why?'
    *'A big boy up the road said he was going to knock
        the stuffing out of me.'*

28. *'Mum, I've knocked the ladder off the side of the
        house.'*
    'Tell your father. I'm busy.'
    'He knows already – he's hanging on to the roof.'

27. *'Mum, Dad's just fallen off the roof.'*
    'I know, dear. I saw him go past the window.'

26. *What is hairy and coughs?*
   A coconut with a cold.

25. *Why did the little ink-spots cry?*
   Because their mother was in a pen doing a long
   sentence.

24. *'Doctor, doctor, I'm only two feet tall.'*
   'You'll just have to be a little patient.'

23. MOTHER: *I've made the chicken soup.*
   FATHER: Thank heavens. I thought it was for us.

22. A small weedy man walked into a pub and
   shouted angrily: 'Who painted my car bright
   pink?'
   An enormous man got up with big rippling
   muscles and said menacingly, 'I did. Why?'

'Oh,' said the small man. 'I thought I'd just tell you the first coat's dry.'

21. MAVIS: *What do you give the man who has everything?*
SANDRA: My telephone number.

20. *'Can you do anything that other people can't?'*
'Yes. I can read my handwriting.'

19. *'It says here that Eskimos eat whale meat and blubber.'*
'You'd blubber too if all you had to eat was whale meat.'

18. *What is five metres tall, green with blue feet and sings like a canary?*
Nothing.

17. BARBER: *Have you been here before? I don't remember your face.*
CUSTOMER: Yes, I have, but it's healed up now.

16. *What must a person be to receive a state funeral?*
Dead.

15. *'These are my golf socks.'*
'Why are they golf socks?'
'They've got 18 holes.'

14. *What's the difference between a soft ball and a hard ball?*
The difference between a lump on the head and concussion.

13. *What's worse than finding a maggot in the strawberry you're eating.*
'Finding half a maggot.

12. *'I just bought my mum a cookbook written in Chinese.'*

'I didn't know she could read Chinese.'

'She can't, but the way she cooks it doesn't matter.'

11. *'This new hearing aid I've got is wonderful. It's so small that nobody notices it.'*

'That's great. How much did it cost?'

'Half past two.'

10. *'Dad, the boy next door said I look just like you.'*

'What did you say?'

'Nothing. He's bigger than me.'

9. *'Doctor, doctor, I keep stealing chairs.'*

'Take a seat.'

8. *What is made of chocolate and lies on the bottom of the sea?'*
An oyster egg.

7. *Which animal never became famous because he got off the wrong train?*
Waterloo Bear.

6. *Who sings 'White Christmas' and explodes?*
Bang Crosby.

5. Did you hear the story of the man who changed his address?
It was a moving story.

4. *Name one Royal photographer.*
Prints Charles.

3. BUTCHER: *Sorry, sir, no ducks today. How about a chicken?*
MAN: Don't be silly. I can't tell my wife I shot a chicken.

2. The teacher noticed that Frank had been staring out of the window for some time, so she decided to catch his attention.

'Frank,' she said, 'if the world is 25,000 miles round and eggs are 62p a dozen, how old am I?'

'Thirty-two,' said Frank.

The teacher blushed and asked: 'How did you know that?'

'Well, my sister's sixteen and she's only half mad.'

1. TEACHER: *What's your name?*
   NEW BOY: Albert Mickey Jones.
   TEACHER: *Then I'll call you Albert Jones.*
   NEW BOY: My dad won't like that.
   TEACHER: *Why not?*
   NEW BOY: He doesn't like people taking the Mickey out of my name.

April fools

The first day of April should be re-named Joker's Day, for it's the one day in the year when every joker can really have fun. On that day, also known as All Fools' Day, I know someone who has returned home to find a room of his house completely emptied of furniture, and who was given brown sauce on ice cream instead of chocolate sauce, cold soup and empty boiled eggs! Yes, that person was me! One year I even got into bed thankful that I hadn't been fooled, and it collapsed!

As a result, I've made a hobby of collecting practical jokes and have started a very special April Fools Campaign which you can join!

April Fools Campaign Manifesto

This is my intention, to see that:

a There is an April Fools Day at least once a month.
b Every person in the world should play at least ten practical jokes every April Fools Day.
c Schools all over the world should begin instructing pupils in how to play practical jokes.
d Custard pies, buckets of water, banana skins and *The Crazy Joker's Handbook* should be prescribed by doctors to anyone feeling sad.
e April Fools Day should be a National holiday.
f By 1990 there should be 365 April Fools Days in every year, and 366 in every leap year!

To join the campaign, simply play as many practical jokes as you can, display the April Fools Campaign poster in your window, and write and tell me your favourite practical jokes. Here are ten of my favourites for you to try out.

Crazy nuts

This is an April Fool that you can play at Christmas! When you have walnuts in the house, break one very carefully down the centre and you will find that it comes perfectly in half. Take out the nut from the inside and replace it with anything you like – a coin, a note on a folded piece of paper, a marble, a chocolate covered nut – absolutely anything that will fit in the shell. Take a spot of glue and stick the two halves back together again so that it looks like a whole nut once more.

Replace it with the other nuts in the bowl, wait for somebody to crack it open and watch the surprise on their faces!

Flying coin

Take a 10p piece and sellotape a piece of cotton thread to it. Lay the coin on the pavement and hide behind a nearby wall or fence, holding the end of the thread. Sooner or later somebody will approach, spot the coin and bend down to pick it up. Just as he reaches down you quickly pull on the cotton and whisk the coin from under his nose.

You'll have to be quick, otherwise the joke might be on you if he gets hold of the coin!

Smashing time

Gather together as many small metal objects as you can – spoons, pieces of chain, tin lids, and so on. One day surprise your mother by offering to do the washing up. Get her to sit down and put her feet up, while you disappear into the kitchen.

After a few minutes, drop the pieces of metal on to the kitchen floor and shout: 'Whoops!'

From where your mother is sitting it will sound like broken crockery, and you will be able to fool her for a long time that you have broken her favourite china!

Phoney phive pounds

Imagine someone's excitement at walking down an empty street and finding a five-pound note lying on the pavement. The finder's mind would start working overtime as to what he could spend it on! Imagine his horror too when he discovers that it isn't a real five-pound note at all but an April fool!

To play this joke you will need a real five-pound note to start with. It might be an idea to let an adult (with a five-pound note) in on this joke too, as they can be a great help to you! All you need to do is get the adult to photocopy the note. There are photocopying machines in libraries and post offices everywhere now, so it should be easy.

When you get the photocopy, cut it out carefully and with some water paints give it a very thin coat of blue paint so that it looks the colour of a five-pound note. When the paint is completely dry, screw the 'note' into a ball and then straighten it out again. If this copy is laid on the ground it will look very much like a real note and it won't be until the victim picks it up that he will realise it isn't.

Write on the back of the note 'Ever been had?' and stick it to the pavement with a piece of blutac so that it doesn't blow away, then sit back and watch what happens.

Come back!

Next time you are parting from a friend and have said goodbye, let him get a few metres away and then call him back. When he comes back to see what you want, lean towards him confidentially and say: 'How far would you have got if I hadn't called you back?'

Alternatively, if he leaves by bicycle stop him and say: 'Did you know your front wheel's going round?'

Sock it to them

Use the longest sock you can find for a really funny practical joke. By using the frame of an old purse (or you can buy one from any craft or needlework shop) you can make an amusing and amazing purse to keep your money in. Simply sew the frame to the top of the sock, and if you push the sock up from the bottom you can make it look like a perfectly ordinary purse.

When you go in a shop to buy something, take out the purse and to the assistant's amazement it will suddenly turn into a sock! It will look incredibly funny as you reach into the toe of a sock to find your money.

Big head!

Did you know that African witch doctors can shrink human heads until they are the size of a tennis ball? Well, you can amaze your friends with your own shrunken head. Peel a large apple and then carve it into the shape of a human head, giving it eye sockets, a nose, a mouth and ears. It doesn't have to be very convincing, but just make it resemble a head.

Leave the apple in a warm place for a few days, and it will dry out and shrivel up to look like a shrunken head. Tease some wool and put it on the top to look like hair, then take the head to school in a little box and tell your friends that your father brought the head back from headhunters!

Pocketful of rye

Take an old school blazer or jacket and sew a plastic or polythene bag into it so that the pocket has a waterproof lining. You can get an adult to do this for you if you cannot sew yourself.

Wearing your special jacket, go out with your friends for a glass of lemonade. Once you have got your drink, astonish everyone around by saying loudly: 'I don't think I'll drink it now. I'll save it for later.'

Then pour the drink casually into your pocket. You can pour it out again later by taking your jacket off carefully and keeping it upright.

Don't forget which is the waterproof pocket, because if you pour it in the wrong one you will get a very wet leg!

When you have a pocketful of drink take care too not to bump into anyone or press up against the pocket, otherwise there could be a big and unexpected splash. You can only do this if you are wearing old clothes that do not matter if they get wet, in which case you could have two waterproof pockets full of *water*. With your hands full of books, ask somebody if they would reach in your pocket to get out your pencil for you!

Crazy cactus

Tell your teacher that your mother collects rare plants and that she is growing some very special cacti. The next day take your teacher one of these cacti as a present. This is really a scouring pad stuck in a small pot of earth, but unless your teacher is a real expert, he or she could start watering this rare specimen.

Reward!

Make some little notes to put through the doors of the houses in your neighbourhood, saying:

> REWARD! REWARD! REWARD!
> Lost on Friday last a green cat
> answering to the name of Olive.
> A £10 reward will be paid to anyone
> finding this beloved pet.

Put your address on the bottom, and you'll be surprised how many people will tell you that they've spotted your 'missing' pet. Make the pet as outrageous as possible – a three-humped camel, a one-legged dog, a two-headed snake – and you'll still find someone who says they think they've seen it!

The last laugh

This is an excellent visual joke to perform during a comedy show or at a concert.

When the show begins you are seen sitting on a chair soaking your feet in a bowl of water. Splash them around a little so that the audience realise that there really is water in the bowl.

Someone can then come on stage and tell you to move because a show is about to be performed. Slowly take your feet out of the bowl and dry them carefully on a towel. Pick up the bowl of water and walk out of the room with it.

At intervals during the show you can simply walk across the stage, still carrying your bowl of water, as if you do not know where to empty it.

Finally, you will walk on. Shrug your shoulders and then throw the contents of the bowl all over the audience!

Everyone in the audience will scream with horror, until they suddenly discover that they are not all wet!

When you come on stage the final time with the bowl it will no longer contain water, but will be perfectly dry and full of confetti, or little squares of torn-up newspaper.

Watching the audience's reaction when they think that they are going to get wet is simply hilarious!

'Never drink water – it might become habit-forming!'